Withdrawn
Outdated Material

# Sexually Transmitted Diseases

DEMCO

# Sexually Transmitted Diseases

# OTHER BOOKS OF RELATED INTEREST

# Sexually Transmitted Diseases

Louise I. Gerdes, *Book Editor*

Daniel Leone, *President*
Bonnie Szumski, *Publisher*
Scott Barbour, *Managing Editor*
Helen Cothran, *Series Editor*

Contemporary Issues
Companion

**GREENHAVEN
PRESS** ®

**THOMSON**
™
**GALE**

San Diego • Detroit • New York • San Francisco • Cleveland
New Haven, Conn. • Waterville, Maine • London • Munich

LIBRARY OF CONGRESS CATALOGING-IN-PUBLICATION DATA

Sexually transmitted diseases / Louise I. Gerdes, book editor.
   p. cm. — (Contemporary issues companion)
   Includes bibliographical references and index.
   ISBN 0-7377-0836-0 (pbk. : alk. paper) — ISBN 0-7377-0837-9 (hb : alk. paper)
    1. Sexually transmitted diseases. 2. Sexually transmitted diseases—Social aspects. I. Gerdes, Louise I. II. Series.
RC200 .S4953 2003
616.95'1—dc21                                   2002072230

# CONTENTS

# FOREWORD

In the news, on the streets, and in neighborhoods, individuals are confronted with a variety of social problems. Such problems may affect people directly: A young woman may struggle with depression, suspect a friend of having bulimia, or watch a loved one battle cancer. And even the issues that do not directly affect her private life—such as religious cults, domestic violence, or legalized gambling—still impact the larger society in which she lives. Discovering and analyzing the complexities of issues that encompass communal and societal realms as well as the world of personal experience is a valuable educational goal in the modern world.

Effectively addressing social problems requires familiarity with a constantly changing stream of data. Becoming well informed about today's controversies is an intricate process that often involves reading myriad primary and secondary sources, analyzing political debates, weighing various experts' opinions—even listening to firsthand accounts of those directly affected by the issue. For students and general observers, this can be a daunting task because of the sheer volume of information available in books, periodicals, on the evening news, and on the Internet. Researching the consequences of legalized gambling, for example, might entail sifting through congressional testimony on gambling's societal effects, examining private studies on Indian gaming, perusing numerous websites devoted to Internet betting, and reading essays written by lottery winners as well as interviews with recovering compulsive gamblers. Obtaining valuable information can be time-consuming—since it often requires researchers to pore over numerous documents and commentaries before discovering a source relevant to their particular investigation.

Greenhaven's Contemporary Issues Companion series seeks to assist this process of research by providing readers with useful and pertinent information about today's complex issues. Each volume in this anthology series focuses on a topic of current interest, presenting informative and thought-provoking selections written from a wide variety of viewpoints. The readings selected by the editors include such diverse sources as personal accounts and case studies, pertinent factual and statistical articles, and relevant commentaries and overviews. This diversity of sources and views, found in every Contemporary Issues Companion, offers readers a broad perspective in one convenient volume.

In addition, each title in the Contemporary Issues Companion series is designed especially for young adults. The selections included in every volume are chosen for their accessibility and are expertly edited in consideration of both the reading and comprehension levels of the audience. The structure of the anthologies also enhances accessibility. An introductory essay places each issue in context and provides helpful facts such as historical background or current statistics and legislation that pertain to the topic. The chapters that follow organize the material and focus on specific aspects of the book's topic. Every essay is introduced by a brief summary of its main points and biographical information about the author. These summaries aid in comprehension and can also serve to direct readers to material of immediate interest and need. Finally, a comprehensive index allows readers to efficiently scan and locate content.

The Contemporary Issues Companion series is an ideal launching point for research on a particular topic. Each anthology in the series is composed of readings taken from an extensive gamut of resources, including periodicals, newspapers, books, government documents, the publications of private and public organizations, and Internet websites. In these volumes, readers will find factual support suitable for use in reports, debates, speeches, and research papers. The anthologies also facilitate further research, featuring a book and periodical bibliography and a list of organizations to contact for additional information.

A perfect resource for both students and the general reader, Greenhaven's Contemporary Issues Companion series is sure to be a valued source of current, readable information on social problems that interest young adults. It is the editors' hope that readers will find the Contemporary Issues Companion series useful as a starting point to formulate their own opinions about and answers to the complex issues of the present day.

# INTRODUCTION

More than twenty-five diseases are spread primarily through sexual activity. Not including the human immunodeficiency virus (HIV) that leads to AIDS, the most common of these sexually transmitted diseases (STDs) are chlamydia, gonorrhea, syphilis, genital herpes, human papillomavirus (HPV), hepatitis B, trichomoniasis, and bacterial vaginosis. While some STDs, such as syphilis, have declined over the years, others, such as genital herpes, gonorrhea, and chlamydia, continue to spread. As of 2001, one in five people in the United States had contracted an STD, and according to the Centers for Disease Control and Prevention (CDC), 15 million people will contract an STD each year—approximately one-fourth of these new cases will occur among teenagers. STDs can result in severe and sometimes deadly consequences and contribute billions of dollars to the nation's healthcare costs each year. These trends, and the continuing epidemic of HIV, represent a serious threat to the public health.

Although STDs are widespread in the United States, most Americans remain unaware of the risks and consequences. For this reason, the alarming spread of STDs, especially among teenagers, is often called a "hidden" epidemic. According to one study, for example, 74 percent of men and 69 percent of women think the risk of contracting an STD is one in ten or fewer, when in fact authorities predict one in four Americans will get an STD in their lifetime. Moreover, while more than 90 percent of both men and women believe that they have a responsibility to tell their sexual partners if they are infected and claim they would feel comfortable doing so, in reality, those who actually have STDs find discussing them difficult, and only a third of infected men and women said they revealed this fact to their partner before they had sexual intercourse.

Another reason the spread of STDs remains a "hidden" epidemic is that many of those who contract STDs have no symptoms and, therefore, remain undiagnosed. For example, 75 percent of women and 50 percent of men with chlamydia, the most commonly reported infectious disease in the United States, have no symptoms. Although easily cured with antibiotics, millions of cases go untreated, and up to 40 percent of women with untreated chlamydia will develop pelvic inflammatory disease (PID). One in five of these women with PID will become infertile. Increased efforts to screen and treat women for chlamydia has resulted in a decline in this devastating STD. However, levels of diseases such as chlamydia remain high, especially among teens.

Once detected, chlamydia, gonorrhea, and syphilis can be cured with antibiotics. However, other STDs such as HIV, genital herpes, hepatitis B, and HPV are viral infections that as yet have no cure. In its 2000 report, *Tracking the Hidden Epidemics: Trends in STDs in the United States*, the CDC reveals that more than 65 million people in the United States are living with an incurable STD, and approximately 7.5 million become infected with an incurable STD each year. Not only must those who become infected with these STDs deal with the direct costs of the care needed to treat and manage their disease, but they must also endure the indirect costs—the pain and suffering, social stigma, and diminished quality of life.

Arguably, those who contract an incurable STD after consenting to sex with partners they know have the disease must accept the consequences of their actions. However, questions about recourse and responsibility arise when people are infected by others who knew or should have known they had an STD and failed to disclose this information. While STDs continue to spread, legal authorities struggle to find the best remedies for these innocent victims. Legal redress can be pursued in either civil or criminal cases.

If victims who contract an incurable STD want to receive compensation in the form of money damages from the individual who infected them, they must pursue a civil remedy according to the laws of their state. In civil cases, the victim, usually with the help of an attorney, brings the case to court as a plaintiff. Criminal cases, on the other hand, are brought on behalf of the people by the state or federal government. Although crimes are often committed against individuals, they are considered offenses against society. Those found guilty in criminal cases often pay for their actions by imprisonment, rather than in monetary damages. Because the law considers imprisonment a greater restriction on the rights of the individual than payment of money damages, the amount, or level, of proof required is greater in criminal cases than in civil suits. For example, in criminal cases, the judge or jury must believe "beyond a reasonable doubt" that a defendant is guilty. In civil cases, they must only believe that a "preponderance" of the evidence proves liability. For this reason proving liability in civil cases may be somewhat easier than proving guilt in criminal cases.

Protecting the public health has always been an aim of the nation's legal system in creating both civil liability and criminal laws. In 1873 American courts established a legal precedent requiring those who have knowledge of an infectious disease to warn others. The Massachusetts Supreme Court in *Minor v. Sharon* held a landlord liable for damages when he allowed tenants to rent a room infected with smallpox. The court said the landlord's knowledge of the danger created a duty to refrain from renting a room he knew to be dangerous, claiming it was a "plain duty of humanity." In 1917, the courts extended this duty to those who transmitted STDs. A Delaware court in *State v. Lankford* held a man liable for infecting his wife with syphilis when he had knowledge of his infection. In the 1950s, after penicillin was discovered to successfully treat bacterial STDs, the incidence of STDs such as syphilis and gonorrhea declined as did lawsuits against those who knowingly transmitted these diseases. However, in the 1980s, with the appearance of AIDS and the increase in cases of genital herpes, HPV, and other incurable STDs, litigation against those who failed to disclose their STDs to sexual partners who contracted these diseases began to increase.

The courts have used several legal theories to impose civil liability on those who transmit STDs, including battery, fraud, and intentional infliction of emotional distress. A "battery" is a harmful or offensive intentional contact with another. If the plaintiff has been touched, intentionally, in a way that he or she has not consented to and that is not in some way justified, the result is a battery. The courts have determined that when an individual knows or should know that he or she is infected with an STD, the intent to inflict harm can be inferred from that individual's failure to disclose the disease to his or her sexual partners. The court in *State v. Lankford* argued that a husband who knows he has syphilis and conceals this fact from his wife who then contracts the disease "inflicts on her physical abuse, and injury, resulting in great bodily harm; and he becomes, notwithstanding his marital rights, guilty of an assault, and indeed, a completed battery." Although the victim consents to the sex, he or she does not consent to be exposed to the disease.

Liability based on fraud is another legal remedy available to victims who contract an incurable STD from sexual partners who know they are infected. In *Kathleen K. v. Robert B.*, a California court held that the defendant's knowledge that he was infected with genital herpes was a material fact that should have been disclosed to protect his sexual partner from injury, and his failure to disclose this fact amounted to a representation that no disease existed. Silence by a defendant who knows he or she is infected is considered a false representation, or fraud.

A relatively new civil remedy available to victims is known as the intentional infliction of emotional distress. To recover damages against a defendant for this claim, the victim must show that the defendant intentionally or recklessly inflicted severe emotional distress on him or her, that the conduct was extreme and outrageous, exceeding "all bounds of decency" and "utterly intolerable in a civilized community," and that the conduct caused the victim's distress. In *B.N. v. K.K.*, a physician infected his girlfriend with genital herpes. The Maryland court held that even if the defendant did not intend to cause the victim emotional distress, it was reasonably foreseeable that she would be emotionally distressed when she became infected with an incurable STD such as genital herpes. The court found the physician liable.

In all of the above civil remedies, the victim must prove that the defendant knew he or she had an STD, which is often the most difficult element to prove. The victim must show that the defendant either desired to infect or knew he or she had an incurable disease that could be transmitted through sexual contact. However, to avoid being held liable to a victim for lack of knowledge, simply not having obtained a medical diagnosis of an STD is insufficient. Some courts have held that having symptoms of an STD or knowledge that a previous sexual partner has an STD is sufficient to establish knowledge. Unfortunately for some victims, many STDs, such as HPV, have no symptoms, or remain symptom-free for a long period, which is true in cases of HIV. Moreover, those infected with incurable STDs do not necessarily know how or under what circumstances their diseases might be transmitted.

Since civil liability in the form of money damages is often insufficient to protect victims who contract incurable STDs with latent symptoms, several states have sought to criminalize the failure to disclose STD infection. Moreover, incurable diseases such as herpes and HIV are considered more offensive and dangerous to society. Because having herpes is not fatal, however, many states do not believe criminal sanctions are necessary. HIV, on the other hand, is a deadly STD, and many states have imposed criminal sanctions to protect society by deterring individuals from transmitting this disease to innocent third parties.

Since the early 1980s, when the public became aware of the deadly consequences of AIDS, many states have enacted criminal statutes that require those with HIV to warn their sexual partners of their HIV status or refrain from conduct that is likely to transmit the disease. States are imposing penalties as significant as life imprisonment for those who are convicted of violating these statutes. At the end of 2000, fourteen states had enacted "partner notification statutes."

Those in favor of criminal liability argue that the purpose behind these statutes is to deter the spread of HIV. In 1905, the U.S. Supreme Court, in *Jacobson v. Massachusetts*, upheld public health laws, arguing that the states have a duty to enact laws to protect the health of their citizens. However, these laws must not unreasonably interfere with the individual's right to care for his or her own body. This individual freedom, on the other hand, is itself subject to restrictions and must be balanced with the safety of the common good. If a state statute bears a reasonable relationship to a legitimate state interest in protecting the health of its citizens, its constitutionality is likely to be upheld.

The state interest being promoted by enacting HIV statutes is the deterrence of the spread of AIDS. Authorities argue that when HIV-positive individuals do not disclose their status, their sexual partners do not have adequate information to make an informed decision about the risks of engaging in sexual relations with that person. Disclosure statutes criminalize the failure to disclose, therefore encouraging HIV-positive individuals to reveal their HIV status to their sexual partners.

However, some authorities believe that criminalizing the act of exposing a person to the HIV virus intrudes into the private lives of HIV-positive citizens and is therefore unconstitutional. These legal analysts claim that a state's interest in protecting the public health is outweighed by an individual's constitutional rights. For example, a statute is considered unconstitutionally vague when it fails to give people of "ordinary intelligence" an opportunity to know what is being prohibited. Statutes must give citizens explicit rules to follow. Some authorities claim that Arkansas's partner notification law fails to provide explicit language about what activities are likely to transfer the HIV virus. In Arkansas, an HIV-positive person can be convicted of exposing another person to HIV through "parenteral transfer of blood." Some legal authorities argue that the language of the statute could be misunderstood by the public, who may not understand the meaning of "parenteral," and claim that the statute is, therefore, unconstitutional.

Another relevant constitutionally protected right was established in the landmark U.S. Supreme Court case of *Roe v. Wade*, which encompassed within the right to privacy the right to personal privacy in marriage, procreation, contraception, and family relationships. Some legal theorists claim that partner notification statutes might be constitutionally invalid because they constitute an invasion of privacy. For example, North Dakota's partner notification statute requires those who are diagnosed HIV-positive to use a prophylactic device when engaging in sexual intercourse. Some might challenge that this requirement limits individual liberty and therefore violates marriage, procreation, and contraceptive rights. However, because courts continue to rule that states have a strong interest in preserving human life and protecting people who are threatened by HIV exposure, as of 2001, no court has found a state's interest in partner notification outweighed by an individual's constitutional rights.

While some analysts argue that partner notification laws are unconstitutional, others are concerned that such statutes are based on erroneous assumptions about the sexual conduct of HIV-positive individuals and are therefore ineffective in deterring the spread of AIDS. Some authorities claim that disclosure statutes actually deter HIV testing, which results in the spread of HIV and AIDS. To avoid the resulting social stigma, rejection, and loss of sexual freedom that may come with being forced by a criminal statute to disclose their HIV status, those at risk for HIV may avoid testing. Obviously, if the statutes deter HIV testing, then the benefit to the public health is not achieved.

Harlon L. Dalton, a professor at Yale Law School and Assistant Director of Law, Policy & Ethics at the university's Center for Interdisciplinary Research on AIDS, also questions whether criminal statutes are an effective means of curbing sexual risk taking. He points out that until policy makers understand what motivates people who are living with HIV to have unprotected sex, they will not know whether these statutes are effective. Dalton cites, for example, the case of Fabian Bridges, an HIV-positive gay man whose "sexual irresponsibility" was documented in a nationally televised PBS documentary. Despite his diagnosis, Bridges had sex with several men in exchange for money. Dalton explains that at first, observers would likely see Bridges as an uncaring victim-turned-victimizer, but on closer inspection, they might sympathize with him. After all, his family abandoned him, and Bridges prostituted himself because he had no other source of money. When a member of Houston's gay community tracked Bridges down and offered him shelter, financial support, and a network of caring people, Bridges no longer needed to put others at risk. Dalton claims that Bridges's story raises questions about the assumptions both legislators and courts make when criminalizing risky sex. HIV-positive individuals who do not inform their partners of their status do not necessarily act out of the callousness, indifference, or malice associated with criminal intent.

Moreover, Dalton argues, HIV-positive individuals are not necessarily conscious of the risk they pose and, therefore, cannot always rationally choose to obey the law. As a condition of receiving federal funds to provide voluntary HIV testing, clinics must provide pre-test and post-test counseling. However, Dalton questions whether this counseling is effective in preventing infected people from engaging in risky behavior. He points out that the news that an individual has tested positive for HIV most likely turns that individual's world upside down: "Facing the prospect of a drastically foreshortened life, a painful death, diminished capacity, loss of control (over virtually everything from one's own body to one's future), shattered dreams, ruptured relationships, social stigma, and abandonment by those whose support an individual needs most—facing the prospect of all this is not, to say the least, easy." Dalton explains that many who test positive for HIV may employ several strategies that human beings use to cope under stressful and traumatic circumstances. Some may compartmentalize, deny, or repress their HIV status to avoid facing social stigma and the threat of death.

The CDC itself notes in its May 1994 *HIV Counseling, Testing, and Referral Guidelines* that the mental confusion and stress that follow a positive test may drown out even the most skillful post-test counseling. It says, "Counselors should recognize that the emotional impact of learning about an HIV-positive test result often prevents clients from absorbing other information during this encounter." Not only is it possible that HIV-positive individuals deny their status to some degree, but many probably cannot absorb the information about the transmission of the disease provided by counselors. Dalton concludes that lawmakers may be inaccurate in assuming that when HIV-positive individuals engage in sexual conduct they are aware of the risk they pose and rationally chose to obey or disobey the law.

Whether criminal partner notification statutes effectively deter the spread of HIV and AIDS or whether civil liability is an adequate remedy to protect victims from intentional exposure to incurable STDs, the STD epidemic remains a significant threat to public health. Authorities continue to debate the most effective strategies for responding to the problem. In articles ranging from scientific studies and surveys to editorials and personal accounts, the authors of *Sexually Transmitted Diseases: Contemporary Issues Companion* examine the nature and scope of the STD epidemic, and the treatment and prevention strategies being implemented to combat these insidious and sometimes deadly diseases.

# CHAPTER 1

# THE NATURE OF SEXUALLY TRANSMITTED DISEASES

Contemporary Issues
Companion

# The Silent STD Epidemic: An Overview

Susan Burner Bankowski and Brandon Bankowski

According to Susan Burner Bankowski and Brandon Bankowski in the following selection, sexually transmitted diseases (STDs) affect millions of people worldwide. However, because of the social stigma associated with STDs, many people are unaware of the nature of these diseases or the scope of their risk. The authors write that the more common STDs include chlamydia, gonorrhea, syphilis, genital herpes, hepatitis B, and AIDS. Chlamydia is the most common STD and is easily treated with antibiotics, but women who contract the disease do not know they have it because they often experience no symptoms until the disease has caused substantial damage to their reproductive systems. However, the authors write, STDs like chlamydia are preventable. For this reason, the authors recommend programs that educate the public on effective ways to prevent STDs as well as screening and reporting programs to help control the spread of these debilitating diseases. Susan Burner Bankowski is associate director of Campaign for Our Children, a national nonprofit organization dedicated to creating educational media campaigns that encourage healthy sexual behavior among youth. Brandon Bankowski is resident physician in the Department of Obstetrics and Gynecology at Johns Hopkins Hospital in Baltimore.

With the pervasive use of sex as a marketing tool and the romanticizing of "worry-free sex" in magazines, on television, and in the movies, it is easy to see why sexual promiscuity has increased greatly over the past 50 years. But the tragedy that generally goes unpublicized is the accompanying rampant spread of sexually transmitted diseases (STDs).

These diseases affect millions of people worldwide. But because they have historically carried a stigma and have been associated with shame, STDs have been largely absent from public discussion. With

From "Let's Face the Silent Epidemic of STDs," by Susan Burner Bankowski and Brandon Bankowski, *The World & I*, June 1999. Copyright © 1999 by *The World & I*. Reprinted with permission.

the advent of AIDS (acquired immune deficiency syndrome) in the 1980s, public awareness of STDs has increased, but there is still far too little known about them. For the most part, STDs are a silent epidemic.

It now appears that, on a global level, at least 1 in 4 persons will contract an STD at some point in his or her life. More than 12 million Americans, including 3 million teenagers, are infected with an STD each year. In the United States alone, as many as 56 million adults and adolescents may already have a lifetime incurable viral STD other than the human immunodeficiency virus (HIV), which leads to AIDS. Moreover, when it comes to contracting curable STDs, this nation has the highest incidence in the developed world.

Many STDs occur without symptoms, are more severe in women, and often go undetected until permanent damage has occurred. If left untreated, they can lead to long-term complications, including severe pain, infertility, birth defects, various cancers and other diseases, and even death. Young adults are at greatest risk of acquiring STDs, for reasons that include having many sexual partners, partners who are more likely to have an infection, and lower use of contraceptives. As well, the public and private costs of STDs are immense. Conservative estimates of total costs are around $10 billion in the United States, rising to $17 billion if HIV infections are included.

Fortunately, STDs are preventable. The problem is that most people don't know much about them, and this lack of knowledge leads to so many infections that could have been prevented.

## √ The Two Most Common Infections √

A young married woman goes to the doctor for a routine checkup. It has been over a year since her last exam. She and her husband have been trying to conceive a child for the past few months but without success. She's not worried, though.

"Everything OK?" she asks assumingly. No, everything is not all right. The doctor informs the woman that she has contracted a sexually transmitted disease called chlamydia.

"That's not possible," she says. "I'm married and my husband doesn't have it. Besides, wouldn't I be able to feel it or see it?" The doctor proceeds to explain that one of them may have contracted the infection recently or could have harbored it for a long time without any symptoms. Either way, she has been infected with a bacterial species that has caused her to have a condition known as PID (pelvic inflammatory disease), which may render her unable to bear children.

Chlamydia and gonorrhea are the most common of all sexually transmitted diseases, with an estimated four million new cases of chlamydia and one million new cases of gonorrhea in the United States each year. Actually, chlamydia is the most common communicable disease in all developed countries, and it is the fastest spreading STD in the United States.

Chlamydia and gonorrhea often occur simultaneously and are similar in many ways. Both are bacterial infections, the causative agents being *Chlamydia trachomatis* and *Neisseria gonorrhoeae*, respectively. They are spread by contact with infected body fluids, such as semen and vaginal secretions, or with mucous membranes, such as those lining the mouth, vagina, and rectum. Between 25 and 40 percent of women who have gonorrhea also have chlamydia.

Gonorrhea, also referred to as "the clap" or "the drip," leads to a puslike discharge from the penis or cervix. It also causes pain in the lower abdomen and a painful, burning sensation when urinating. But among women, 30–80 percent of infections are asymptomatic, while for men that figure is below 5 percent. Chlamydia is less obvious and trickier to detect: As many as 85 percent of infected women and about 40 percent of infected men have no symptoms.

In infected women, when symptoms such as lower belly pain do occur, it is often because the bacteria have permanently scarred the woman's reproductive system. This damage may lead to infertility or a dangerous ectopic pregnancy—that is, the fetus may start growing outside the uterus. Alternatively, even if the pregnancy is carried to term, both diseases can be transmitted to the baby during vaginal delivery, causing eye infections and chronic pneumonia in newborns. It is therefore very important for a pregnant woman to obtain prenatal testing and care. Both infections can be cured with one dose of antibiotics taken orally.

## The Stages of Syphilis

A young man notices that the palms of his hands have acquired a rash that persists for several days, no matter what creams or lotions he applies. A week or two later, at the insistence of his girlfriend, he decides to go to the doctor. After running some blood tests, the physician informs him that the rash is a symptom of syphilis that has spread throughout his body. Explaining the risks involved with the disease, the doctor recommends that he and his girlfriend get treated immediately. The young man is surprised, saying that he never noticed any symptoms "down there." But he is also fearful, so he takes the doctor's advice and accepts treatment.

There are around 120,000 new cases of syphilis in the United States each year. The disease, which is caused by the bacterial species *Treponema pallidum*, affects the body in stages. The first stage is characterized by a painless, hard, red sore called a *chancre*, which appears at the site where the person is first infected—often the mouth, penis, or vagina. The sore may be as small as a pimple or as large as a dime. After several weeks, the chancre "resolves" (disappears), but that doesn't mean that the disease is gone. Direct contact with one of these lesions will transmit the bacteria to another person. The infectious agent may also be transmitted to a fetus through the placenta. At this stage, syphilis may be easily treated with an antibiotic such as penicillin.

If untreated, the patient generally develops secondary or "disseminated" syphilis, roughly six months after the initial sore has cleared up. This stage may be recognized by a flaking, nonitchy rash on the palms of the hands, the soles of the feet, or all over the body. Other symptoms may include fever, weight loss, and swollen lymph nodes. This stage may last several weeks to months, but it will also go away on its own.

If the infection is still not treated, tertiary syphilis may occur, which can permanently damage the brain, eyes, bones, or heart and may even lead to death. If caught in time, this stage requires weeks of hospitalization and treatment with drugs given intravenously. The damage is often irreversible.

## A Recurrent Virus

A pregnant woman traveling far from home suddenly goes into labor and is rushed to a hospital. The obstetrician, unfamiliar with her medical history, asks her a number of questions, including whether she's had any STD in the past. She says she once had herpes but doesn't have it now. Luckily, the doctor examines her cervix and vagina, for her cervix has a herpes sore of which she was unaware. The doctor then delivers the baby by cesarean section, to prevent the child from contacting the sore and getting a potentially brain-damaging infection.

In the United States alone, about 40 million people have been infected with the herpes simplex virus (HSV), and 300,000–500,000 new cases are reported each year. The virus, which has two common strains (HSV types 1 and 2), causes painful sores around the mouth and on the genitals. Any touching of a herpes sore may transmit the virus to another person or another part of one's own body, including the eyes.

The sores generally last two to three weeks before going away on their own. But half the number of infected people get recurrent outbreaks of the painful sores for many years, potentially for the rest of their lives. Some studies have shown that herpes increases a woman's risk for cervical cancer. There is no cure for herpes, but expensive antiviral medicines may decrease the symptoms or shorten the duration of the outbreaks.

If a baby is delivered during an active outbreak of the disease, it can acquire a deadly brain infection known as meningitis. An outbreak may be hard to detect because the lesions are often inside the vagina or on the cervix. Babies should be delivered by cesarean section if the mother has active herpes.

## The Preventable Virus

The doctor who prescribed antibiotic treatment for the young woman with chlamydia follows up with a recommendation that she get a vaccine against hepatitis as well. "But why would I need that?" she protests. The doctor explains that people who have an STD are at greater risk for hepatitis B as well, because their sexual partners could very likely carry other infections and because any lesions will make transmission easier.

Hepatitis B is a dangerous virus that attacks the liver. About 200,000 people get "hep B" each year. It is contracted through oral, vaginal, or anal intercourse, sharing drug needles or other piercing equipment, or being exposed to infected blood. If a person gets the virus, it may take up to five months before causing a flulike syndrome, with nausea, vomiting, stomach pain, and headaches. As the disease progressively destroys the liver, the patient's skin may turn yellow (a condition called jaundice) and he may become very ill.

Often the infection resolves on its own in one or two months, but some people remain chronically infected—that is, the disease remains in their system. Most of the latter cases show no symptoms, but the virus can still be transmitted to other people. In about 4 percent of cases, the infection is fatal. Treatment of an active case of the disease may involve complicated, multidrug therapy.

Hepatitis B is the only STD for which there is a vaccine: A series of three shots prevents a person from contracting the disease. If you think you may be at risk, or if your sexual partner has hepatitis, ask your doctor to test you for the virus.

## HIV: An Insidious Agent

The bus is crowded with the usual group of morning passengers. A teenage boy, riding to high school, recognizes many of the faces. As his eyes scan the advertisements along the side of the bus, they stop at a new ad that reads, "48 teens were infected with HIV . . . today." He looks at the others riding to school with him and wonders which of his friends may already have been infected. There's no way he can tell just by looking at them.

The human immunodeficiency virus (HIV) is an insidious agent that gradually weakens and destroys a person's immune system. As a result, someone who has been infected with the virus for a long time readily succumbs to infections by other pathogens. These "opportunistic" infections lead to diseases that are collectively known as AIDS. Thus, while HIV itself does not kill the patient, the development of AIDS does.

Roughly a million people in the United States have HIV, and 45,000 more contract the virus each year via sexual contact, shared needles, contact with infected blood, and breast-feeding. Women are the fastest-growing segment of the infected population. Worldwide, 75 percent of HIV infections stem from sexual activity, 10 percent result from intravenous drug use, and 10 percent are vertically transmitted from infected mother to baby. Eighty percent of the sexually transmitted HIV occurs by heterosexual contact. Someone who has had other STDs is at increased risk of getting HIV.

People infected with HIV often show no symptoms for weeks or months. The first evidence of the disease may be a flulike illness that occurs when the patient undergoes "sero-conversion"—that is, when the virus can be detected in the blood by a lab test. It may take six months from the time of infection before the tests give a positive result. This means that someone whose test result is negative may still have HIV and be able to transmit the infection to someone else.

HIV is a slow-acting but complicated virus. Because it frequently mutates inside the patient's body, it is quite difficult to treat. As the infection progresses, the amount of virus in the bloodstream increases, while the number of "CD4" immune cells (which are attacked by the virus) decreases. At present, there is no cure for the infection, but the patient may need to take up to 18 pills a day to fight the infection and prolong his life. These medications (called antiretrovirals) are not only expensive but may have strong side effects that make the person feel very ill.

An HIV-infected woman can transmit the virus to her child during pregnancy or when breast-feeding. Certain drug therapies, called ZDV or AZT, can greatly reduce the risk of transmission during pregnancy. It is also recommended that HIV-positive women deliver via cesarean section and when their "viral load" (concentration of virus in the blood) is low, but both these approaches are still being investigated. In addition, an HIV-positive woman should avoid breast-feeding, unless, as in some developing countries that have high infant mortality rates, the deprivation of breast milk with its natural immunities would be life threatening to the child.

In addition to the aforementioned infections, there are many other STDs that are harrowing if not just as threatening. They include trichomoniasis (a parasitic infection), pubic lice, scabies, chancroid, and human papillomavirus, the last of which often causes genital warts and may further cause penile and cervical cancers.

## Preventing STDs

We need to remind ourselves that STDs are preventable. Effective prevention should include both individual education and population-based approaches. Whether the education consists of a one-on-one dialogue, classroom-style lecturing, or mass-media dissemination, it enables individuals to make informed decisions and protect themselves from these diseases by changing risky behaviors. Good STD-prevention education needs to include several vital components:

• Knowledge of the disease, conveying the mode of transmission, the symptoms, and the treatment. It is important to note that disappearance of the symptoms does not mean that the disease has been cured and cannot be transmitted to others. Also, many STDs are transmitted in ways other than sexual intercourse.

• Abstinence-based education, which emphasizes that the safest way to avoid contracting an STD is not to engage in sexual activity outside of a mutually faithful relationship. Remember, it is impossible to tell if a person is disease free by simply looking at him or her, and a potential partner may be symptom free but still harbor an infection.

• The understanding that while certain STDs are curable, others are not. The problem is complicated by the emergence of strains of pathogenic microbes that are resistant to antibiotics.

• The knowledge that it is safest for both partners to be tested for all STDs before having sex, regardless of whether they plan on using "barrier methods" such as condoms or dental dams.

• Stressing the importance of maintaining a monogamous relationship once the partners have been tested.

• Education about the dangers of intravenous drug use and needle sharing.

In addition to education and counseling, critical components of population-based prevention and control include: (1) screening high-risk populations for prevalent STDs; (2) treating individuals with diagnosed and probable infections; and (3) reporting STD cases to the Health Department.

These approaches are extremely important for many reasons. Foremost is the health and well-being of the population. Better knowledge about STDs will reduce their transmission and result in fewer people becoming infected. In addition, screening and knowledge about risks and symptoms will reduce the degree of long-term damage to infected individuals. On a policy level, prevention and early treatment are cost effective. It is far less expensive to prevent a disease than to treat it, and the early stages of infection are not as costly to treat as the more advanced stages.

In conclusion, sexually transmitted diseases silently impair the lives and futures of millions of people each year worldwide. Although all STDs are preventable and many are curable, they impose enormous social, physical, and financial burdens on individuals and on society as a whole. Advocacy and funding for education, screening, treatment, reporting, and behavior modification must be continued in order to stop this epidemic and reduce the rates of sexually transmitted infections.

# CHLAMYDIA: THE MOST COMMON BACTERIAL STD

John S. Williamson and Christy M. Wyandt

According to John S. Williamson and Christy M. Wyandt, chlamydia is the most commonly reported infectious disease. In the following selection, the authors explain that the characteristic of chlamydia that poses the greatest obstacle to controlling the spread of the disease is that it often produces no symptoms, especially in women. However, when left untreated, the disease can spread to the reproductive system, increasing the risk of pelvic inflammatory disease (PID), which can lead to chronic pelvic pain, ectopic pregnancies, and infertility. For this reason, the authors suggest that communities adopt screening programs that have proven effective in controlling the spread of the disease. Williamson and Wyandt are with the Department of Medicinal Chemistry and the Department of Pharmaceutics at the Research Institute of Pharmaceutical Sciences and the National Center for the Development of Natural Products, School of Pharmacy, University of Mississippi.

According to the Centers for Disease Control & Prevention (CDC), an estimated 333 million new cases of curable sexually transmitted diseases (STDs) occur throughout the world each year among adults. While much progress has been made in STD prevention, the United States still has the highest incidence of STDs in the industrialized world. It is easily 50 to 100 times higher, although the occurrence of gonorrhea and syphilis has recently been brought to historic lows.

The CDC reports that STDs now account for more than 85% of the most common infectious diseases in this country. In addition, there are an estimated 15 million new cases of STDs in the United States annually, approximately two-thirds of which occur in persons under 25 years of age.

## The ABCs of STDs

STDs affect men and women of all backgrounds and economic levels, with the highest prevalence among teens and young adults. Some con-

Excerpted from "Chlamydia: The Silent STD," by John S. Williamson and Christy M. Wyandt, *Drug Topics*, September 4, 2000. Copyright © 2000 by Thomson Medical Economics. Reprinted with permission.

tributing factors in the overall rise of STDs include societal changes—young people becoming sexually active earlier, divorce being more common, and the sexually active being more likely to have multiple partners. STDs disproportionately affect women, minorities, infants, and the young. In women, STDs can lead to pelvic inflammatory disease (PID), infertility, potentially fatal ectopic pregnancies, and cancer of the reproductive tract. STDs can also result in irreparable lifetime damage for infants infected by their mothers during gestation or birth. Such exposure can result in blindness, bone deformities, mental retardation, and even death. Early detection and treatment can be hindered, since many STDs initially show few or no symptoms, especially in women. When symptoms do develop, they may be confused with those of other diseases that are not transmitted through sexual contact. Since STDs can still be transmitted by an asymptomatic carrier, an infected individual can unknowingly become an STD "Typhoid Mary" [a person from whom something undesirable or deadly spreads to those nearby]. Other factors that contribute to the uncontrolled spread of STDs include a lack of widespread routine STD screening programs, the social stigma associated with these diseases, and a lack of public awareness concerning STDs. Unfortunately, most STDs remain undiagnosed.

Only three STDs have been classified as nationally reportable diseases: gonorrhea, syphilis, and chlamydia. Health-care providers are required to report each diagnosed case to state health departments and the CDC. There are no national reporting requirements for any of the other five major STDs: genital herpes, human papillomavirus (HPV), hepatitis B, HIV, and trichomoniasis.

The major STDs can be divided into two groups—those that are bacterial in origin and those that are viral in origin. Treatment of bacterial STDs most often results in a cure, with the course of therapy limited and relatively inexpensive. Unfortunately, viral STDs are incurable and often require extended treatment. The greatest costs associated with STDs are those resulting from complications of untreated chlamydia and gonorrhea, those resulting from treatment of precancerous cervical lesions in HPV infection, and treatment of HIV/AIDS.

In a 1998 Kaiser Family Foundation/*Glamour* magazine survey, it was shown that most men and women of reproductive age (18 to 44 years old) seriously underestimate how common STDs are as well as their personal risk for getting an STD. While an estimated one in four Americans will get an STD in their lifetime, the majority of men (74%) and women (69%) think the rate is one in 10 Americans or fewer. Only 14% of men and 8% of women said they think they are at risk for STDs. Two-thirds of single men and women said they do not "always" use condoms. In addition, only one in five teens said they think they are at risk of getting a STD. In a 1995 Gallup Organization poll, over half of adults and over one-third of teens said their health-care providers spend "no time at all" discussing STDs with them. The estimated incidence and costs associated with STDs indicates the great need for general public educational awareness on the topic of sexual health. Using their unique positions in both the community and the clinic, pharmacists are poised to play an essential role in providing patient information to help reduce the spread of STDs and their suffering and costs.

## Topping the List

Chlamydia, tracked for the first time in 1995, has consistently remained the most reported infectious disease, followed by gonorrhea and HIV/AIDS. These three, plus syphilis and hepatitis B, account for 87% of the total number of all medical cases caused by the top 10 maladies, according to a recent report released by the CDC. . . .

Not all of the diseases caused by the chlamydiae [parasites] are sexually transmitted. In fact, chlamydial infections are among the most common of human pathogen infections, with a 50% to 70% positive age-specific sero-prevalence rate [the rate at which a population tests positive] in the world's population. Taking into account that individuals lose antibody over time, it is quite possible that almost all humans have some exposure to these organisms at some time in their lives. The chlamydiae are known to cause a wide range of human diseases and are currently implicated in the causation of others, such as asthma and atherosclerosis [when fatty deposits are found inside the arterial walls]. In their natural hosts, it is common for chlamydial infections to result in only relatively mild diseases. However, relatively poor host immunity results in recurrent infections. Serious consequences associated with chlamydia infection are well documented but tend to occur relatively late in the course of the disease.

Interestingly, diseases associated with the chlamydiae can be traced back to ocular infections described in ancient Chinese documents as well as in the Ebers papyrus of Egypt thousands of years ago. One such disease, trachoma, which is caused by *Chlamydia trachomatis* infection, continues to be a major cause of preventable blindness, with an estimated 500 million cases of active trachoma worldwide. Only during the 1980s and 1990s has genital chlamydial infection been identified as a major public health problem. This is due to the association of the genital infection with disease syndromes such as nongonococcal urethritis, mucopurulent cervicitis, PID, ectopic pregnancy, and tubal infertility. The World Health Organization (WHO) estimates that 90 million new cases of genital chlamydial infections occur worldwide each year. This translates to an estimated 5 million new cases in the United States each year, with 50,000 women becoming infertile as a result. . . .

Genital infections due to *Chlamydia trachomatis* are the most common STDs in the United States. These infections present unique problems for public health control programs, since 50% to 70% of these infections in women (and possibly men) are clinically silent. Unrecognized and untreated, the pathogen may remain infectious in the host for months and can be readily transmitted to sex partners. Furthermore, most reported infections occur in the 15–24 age group. Young women with cervical chlamydial infections are at risk for PID, which can lead to long-term reproductive problems, including chronic pelvic pain, ectopic pregnancy, and tubal infertility. In addition, babies born to infected mothers are also at risk for conjunctivitis and pneumonia. The annual direct and indirect costs of genital chlamydial infections in the United States alone have been estimated at more than $2 billion.

## The Complications of Chlamydia

Nongonococcal urethritis (NGU) is a common sexual infection caused by several microorganisms, the most common and most serious of which is *Chlamydia*. NGU is an infection of the urethra, the tube that carries urine from the bladder. In general, NGU is applied to the symptoms that men have, since NGU-type symptoms in women can be the result of many different etiologies. The key NGU symptoms in men include: discharge from the penis, burning at urination, and burning or itching around the opening of the penis. These symptoms occur most frequently in the morning; however, some men will have no symptoms or symptoms so mild that they go unnoticed.

If women become infected with the microorganisms that cause NGU in men, the infections create problems in the reproductive tract more often than in the urethra. And the long-term consequences of these infections tend to be more severe in women. Since the infections are internal and often without noticeable symptoms, it is common for women not to know that they are infected until serious complications occur. Left untreated, the microorganisms that cause NGU can lead to: permanent damage to the reproductive organs of both men and women, resulting in infertility; problems in pregnancy, resulting in premature delivery or low birth weight; and eye, ear, and lung infections in newborns.

Pelvic inflammatory disease (PID) is a serious infection of a woman's reproductive organs and a leading cause of infertility in the United States. Although a variety of microorganisms can cause PID, the most common are chlamydia and gonorrhea. PID occurs when an infection in the genital tract is left untreated long enough to spread from the cervix into the uterus, fallopian tubes, and ovaries. It can develop any time from several days to several months after infection, causing scarring in the fallopian tubes that can lead to tubal pregnancy (a life-threatening pregnancy in which there is no chance of producing a baby). Women who have had PID may experience problems getting pregnant or bearing children; in addition, PID can be the source of long-lasting pain. The most common symptom of PID is dull pain or tenderness in the lower abdomen. Other possible symptoms include: bleeding between menstrual periods, increased or altered vaginal discharge, pain during sex, nausea and/or vomiting, and fever and chills. Unfortunately, many infected women exhibit either no symptoms or symptoms too mild to notice while PID is causing permanent damage.

Most women will have vaginitis at least once in their lifetime. Vaginitis is usually described as itching or burning in the vagina, often with an unusual odor or a discharge. The most common kinds of vaginitis are bacterial vaginosis (BV), yeast, and trichomoniasis (trich). BV is the most common kind of vaginitis and is caused by the rapid growth of several different kinds of bacteria in the vagina. It is not clear exactly why a woman gets BV or why some women recover without treatment while others develop more serious infections. In general, vaginitis is seldom dangerous, and in most women it is easy to treat. The symptoms of bacterial vaginitis include: a strong, fishy odor, especially after sex; a white or gray discharge; or a watery or foamy discharge. Once again, many cases of BV are so mild that women do not realize they are infected. In pregnant women, BV can cause babies to be born early or with low birth weight.

The fetus that is exposed to chlamydia in the birth canal during delivery may develop conjunctivitis (eye infection) or pneumonia. Symptoms of conjunctivitis, which include discharge and swollen eyelids, usually develop within the first 10 days of life. Symptoms of pneumonia, including a progressively worsening cough and congestion, most often develop within three to six weeks of birth. Because of these risks to the newborn, many doctors recommend routine testing of all pregnant women for chlamydial infection. . . .

## Controlling the Spread of Infection

The symptomatic silence of all chlamydial infections is the hallmark of this microorganism. Most infected persons will have mild or no apparent clinical disease symptoms. As previously mentioned, asymptomatic infection not only creates a problem in the detection of the disease but also contributes to the development of long-term adverse problems, such as the scarring trachoma in ocular infection, pelvic inflammatory disease, ectopic pregnancy, and tubal-factor infertility from genital infection. Therefore, early diagnosis is an essential component of any public health program in controlling chlamydial infections. . . .

Studies validate that targeted screening programs to detect cervical chlamydial infection decrease the overall incidence of symptomatic PID. Patients with genital gonococcal or chlamydial infections are also at increased risk for HIV, and although the risk may be lower than in those with genital ulcer disease, the higher prevalence of chlamydial infection suggests that the attributable risk for HIV may be substantially higher for chlamydia. Therefore, shortening the duration of infection by early diagnosis and treatment could have a major impact on risk reduction for HIV infection. . . .

In areas where control programs emphasizing early diagnosis, targeted screening, partner notification, and effective treatment have been implemented, a slow decline in incidence of genital chlamydial infection has been observed. In fact, due to the increased sensitivity of laboratory testing as well as more complete data from widespread screening programs, the true rate of decline may actually be significantly higher than the reported rate. In women, screening for chlamydial infection has been especially successful when coupled with regular Pap testing, prenatal visits, or attendance at family planning or pregnancy counseling clinics.

Coupling the chlamydial screen with other such testing allows the patient to avoid the stigmas associated with STD testing. Asymptomatic men infected with chlamydia are much less likely to access medical care than women. Although asymptomatic men are inherently responsible for a major portion of the spread of this disease, current public health programs do not adequately address these individuals.

# Gonorrhea: A Resistant Bacterium

National Institute of Allergy and Infectious Diseases

In the following selection, the National Institute of Allergy and Infectious Diseases (NIAID), a component of the National Institutes of Health, explains that the potential complications of gonorrhea can be severe and even life-threatening to women and their babies. According to the NIAID, for example, gonorrhea can spread to the uterus, resulting in pelvic inflammatory disease (PID), which in turn can lead to infertility and ectopic pregnancies, in which a fertilized egg implants in the fallopian tubes rather than the uterus. Moreover, the institute reports that the number of strains of gonorrhea that are resistant to antibiotic treatment is increasing. For this reason, the NIAID supports research to find better methods to diagnose, treat, and prevent the disease.

In 1995, 392,848 cases of gonorrhea in the United States were reported to the U.S. Centers for Disease Control and Prevention (CDC). The Institute of Medicine, however, estimates that 800,000 cases of gonorrhea occur annually in the United States. The annual cost of gonorrhea and its complications is estimated at close to $1.1 billion.

Gonorrhea is caused by a bacterium, *Neisseria gonorrhoeae*, that grows and multiplies quickly in moist, warm areas of the body including the reproductive tract, the oral cavity, and the rectum. Although in women the cervix usually is the initial site of infection, the disease can spread to and infect the uterus (womb) and fallopian tubes, resulting in pelvic inflammatory disease (PID). This can cause infertility and ectopic (tubal) pregnancy.

The disease is most commonly spread during sexual intercourse—vaginal, oral, and anal. Gonorrhea of the rectum can occur in people who practice anal intercourse and also may occur in women due to spread of the infection from the vaginal area.

Gonorrhea can be passed from an infected woman to her newborn infant during delivery, causing eye infections in the baby. When the infection occurs in the genital tract, mouth, or rectum of a child, it is due most commonly to sexual abuse.

From "Fact Sheet: Gonorrhea," by the National Institute of Allergy and Infectious Diseases, www.ama-assn.org, June 1998. Copyright © 1998 by the American Medical Association. Reprinted with permission.

## Diagnosing and Treating the Symptoms

The early symptoms of gonorrhea often are mild, and many women who are infected have no symptoms of the disease. If symptoms of gonorrhea develop, they usually appear within two to 10 days after sexual contact with an infected partner, although a small percentage of patients may be infected for several months without showing symptoms. The initial symptoms in women include a painful or burning sensation when urinating and/or vaginal discharge that is yellow or bloody. More advanced symptoms, which indicate progression to PID, include abdominal pain, bleeding between menstrual periods, vomiting, or fever. Men are more often symptomatic than women. They usually have a discharge from the penis and a burning sensation during urination that may be severe. Symptoms of rectal infection include discharge, anal itching, and sometimes painful bowel movements.

Three techniques, gram stain, detection of bacterial genes or nucleic acid (DNA), and culture, are generally used to diagnose gonorrhea. Many doctors prefer to use more than one test to increase the chance of an accurate diagnosis. The gram stain is quite accurate for men but is not very sensitive for women. Only one in two women with gonorrhea have a positive gram stain. The test involves placing a smear of the discharge from the penis or the cervix (the opening to the uterus) on a slide and staining the smear with a dye. The slide is examined under a microscope for the presence of the bacteria. A doctor usually can give test results to the patient at the time of an office or clinic visit. More often, urine or cervical swabs are used for a new test that detects the genes of the bacteria. These tests are as accurate as culture and are used widely.

The culture test involves placing a sample of the discharge onto a culture plate and incubating it up to two days to allow the bacteria to multiply. The sensitivity of this test depends on the site from which the sample is taken. Cervical samples detect infection approximately 90 percent of the time. The doctor also can take a throat culture to detect pharyngeal gonorrhea.

Because penicillin-resistant cases of gonorrhea are common, other antibiotics are used to treat most patients with gonococcal infections. One of the most effective medicines to treat patients is ceftriaxone, which the doctor can inject in a single dose. Other effective antibiotics that a patient can take by mouth include a single dose of cefixime, ciprofloxacin, or ofloxacin. Pregnant women and patients younger than 18 years old should not take ciprofloxacin or ofloxacin.

Gonorrhea can occur together with chlamydial infection, another common sexually transmitted disease (STD). Therefore, doctors usually prescribe a combination of antibiotics, such as ceftriaxone and doxycycline or azithromycin. Single-dose oral therapy is available. All sexual partners of a person with gonorrhea should be tested and treated if infected whether or not they have symptoms of infection.

## The Complications

The most common consequence of untreated gonorrhea is PID, a serious infection of the female reproductive organs that occurs in an estimated 1 million American women each year. Gonococcal PID often appears immediately after the menstrual period. PID can scar or damage cells lining the fallopian tubes, resulting in infertility in as many as 10 percent of women affected. If the tube is only partially scarred, proper passage of the fertilized egg into the uterus is prevented. If this happens, the egg may implant in the tube; this is called ectopic or tubal pregnancy and is life-threatening if not detected early. Rarely, untreated gonorrhea can spread to the blood or the joints.

An infected pregnant woman may give the infection to her infant as the baby passes through the birth canal during delivery. A doctor can prevent infection of the eye, called ophthalmia neonatorum, by applying silver nitrate or other medications to the baby's eyes immediately after birth. Because of the risks from gonococcal infection to both mother and child, doctors recommend that a pregnant woman have at least one test for gonorrhea.

Gonorrhea also increases the risk of HIV infection (HIV, human immunodeficiency virus, causes AIDS), so prevention and early treatment of gonorrhea is critically important.

By using male condoms correctly and consistently during sexual activity, sexually active people can reduce their risk of gonorrhea and its complications.

Scientists supported by the National Institute of Allergy and Infectious Diseases (NIAID) are continuing to learn more about the organism that causes gonorrhea and are working on better methods to prevent, diagnose, and treat it. The dramatic rise of antibiotic-resistant strains of the gonococcus underscores the need for a means of preventing gonorrhea. Scientists have developed a laboratory method to detect these resistant strains, which helps the physician select an appropriate treatment.

An effective vaccine against gonorrhea remains a key research priority for NIAID-supported scientists. Determining the sequence of the bacterial genome is expected to aid scientists in identifying new vaccine candidates.

# SYPHILIS: A DANGEROUS MIMIC

Lisa Marr

In the following selection, taken from her book *Sexually Transmitted Diseases: A Physician Tells You What You Need to Know*, Lisa Marr explains that cases of syphilis declined after the discovery of penicillin, which is used to treat the disease. However, epidemics of syphilis continue to plague certain people in the United States, particularly the poor, she reveals. According to Marr, the symptoms of syphilis vary depending on how far the disease has advanced. For example, an ulcer, or chancre, may appear in the disease's primary stage, while flu-like symptoms may appear in its secondary stage. Unfortunately, says Marr, because the symptoms of syphilis often mimic other diseases, it may go undetected, and without treatment can result in debilitating complications, even brain damage. If detected, however, syphilis can easily be treated with antibiotics, which is why Marr suggests that those at risk should be screened for the disease. Marr has lectured about STDs, taught medical trainees in the field of STDs, and conducted research relating to STDs, particularly herpes.

Syphilis is an infection caused by the bacterium *Treponema pallidum*, which can be transmitted through sexual contact or from mother to child during pregnancy. This bacterium can infect many different organ systems and cause a full range of symptoms. Although antibiotics effectively treat syphilis, the disease is still a major health problem, and epidemics of syphilis still occur in some areas of the United States.

## How Common Is It?
Approximately 50,000 people are diagnosed with syphilis each year in the United States. The number of people infected with syphilis in this country reached a peak in the late 1940s, but with the discovery of penicillin, which was the first successful treatment for syphilis, the number began declining. In the late 1970s and early 1980s there was a resurgence of the disease, the primary reservoir for infection being men who had sex with other men. However, with increased awareness of the human immunodeficiency virus (HIV) and the importance of

safer sex practices among this group, heterosexuals have now become the primary reservoir for infection.

As the incidence of syphilis among heterosexuals rises, more and more infected children are being born to mothers with syphilis. About one child in a thousand born in the United States is infected with the disease. Infection of a newborn can cause devastating, lifelong problems. Syphilis screening is routine for women who obtain prenatal care in the United States, but many women for various reasons do not seek health care, or are excluded from it, and therefore sexually transmitted diseases, including syphilis, are not detected during their pregnancies.

There have been epidemics of syphilis in certain areas of the country, particularly in the South and coastal urban areas, despite an overall decline in the past few years in the number of people infected. In other areas of the world, such as Africa and Southeast Asia, the rates of infection are much higher. People infected with syphilis in the United States in the 1990s are more often the poor, those who use drugs, and those who engage in sex in exchange for drugs. Between 14 and 36 percent of people who are HIV positive are also infected with syphilis; a person with syphilis lesions is more susceptible to becoming infected with HIV.

## What Are the Symptoms?

The symptoms of syphilis are numerous and varied. Any organ system can be affected. Those who have compromised immune systems, such as persons with acquired immunodeficiency syndrome (AIDS), may have a more aggressive course of infection and less typical symptoms.

Syphilis is divided into early and late stages of infection. Early infection is further subdivided into primary syphilis, secondary syphilis, and early latent syphilis. Late infection is also subdivided, into late latent syphilis, tertiary syphilis, and neurosyphilis. How long the infection has been present and the nature of the symptoms determine which stage of infection is present, what type of treatment is necessary, and for how long it must be administered.

After infection with syphilis, symptoms of primary syphilis can take between ten and ninety days to appear, with the average interval being around three weeks. The first symptom is an ulcer, called a *chancre*, which is usually painless. There is usually only one chancre, which occurs at the site where infection took place. This can be on any area of the skin or on any mucous membrane. Rarely, the lesion is slightly painful, especially if there is a secondary infection with skin bacteria.

A swab taken from the chancre is usually seen to contain the syphilis-causing bacterium, *Treponema pallidum*, when examined under the microscope. There is usually a nonpainful swelling of the lymph nodes in the area of the infection. Often the infected person does not realize that he or she is infected, especially since a painless lesion is easy to miss, particularly if it is in the vagina or on the cervix for a woman or in the urethra for a man. The lesion usually disappears on its own after a few weeks without treatment.

## The Later Stages

If a person is not diagnosed and treated at this point, then, several months later, symptoms of secondary syphilis can appear. This stage occurs when the syphilis-causing bacterium enters the bloodstream from the lesion. It can seed any organ and cause a variety of symptoms, including

- A red, flat, nonitching rash over the whole body, including the palms and soles
- Swelling of the lymph nodes throughout the body
- Fever
- Sore throat
- Joint aches
- Headaches
- Patchy hair loss
- Wart-like lesions in the genital area that are not warts but manifestations of secondary syphilis

There can also be painless lesions on the mucous membranes and neurological changes, among other symptoms. People with secondary syphilis may also feel like they have the flu, and in fact these symptoms are so vague that they can easily be mistaken for other medical problems. All of these symptoms will eventually resolve without causing further problems, but this does not mean that the infection has gone away.

During both the primary and secondary phases of syphilis, a person is very infectious to partners. As can be imagined, both phases of the infection are often missed, either because the initial lesion is not noticed or because the symptoms are thought to have another cause, since they are so vague. In addition, since both of these phases are transient, people may think the problem has gone away when the symptoms resolve, but this is not the case. People with infection persisting beyond this point can live for many years, often decades, without experiencing further symptoms. Infection may be detected only through routine blood testing, and it is then called latent syphilis. People are still potentially infectious during this time, especially soon after resolution of the secondary syphilis stage.

The syphilis-causing bacterium can cause destruction of internal organs, a stage known as tertiary syphilis or late syphilis. This stage is rarely seen today, since the discovery of antibiotics has made syphilis so treatable, but virtually any organ system—such as the bones, liver, skin, and heart—can be damaged. If infection progresses to the brain, it is called *neurosyphilis*. In these stages the infection can be life threatening.

Infected newborns may have no symptoms, or the symptoms may

be severe enough to cause brain damage and death. At birth, a child who is infected may not have a positive blood test, for the disease may take several weeks to show up on blood tests; for this reason, children born to high-risk mothers must have follow-up tests performed a few weeks after birth. Symptoms in infected newborns include brain damage, bone deformities, dental malformations, hearing loss, and rash. Women who are pregnant and are infected with syphilis have a higher risk of miscarriage: only 20 percent of women with syphilis will carry a fetus to term and deliver a normal, healthy baby. In the United States and in many other parts of the world, testing for syphilis is a routine part of prenatal health care.

## How Is Syphilis Transmitted?

Syphilis is transmitted through sexual or other intimate contact with an infected person, or from mother to unborn child. A person who has sex with another person who has active syphilis lesions has about a 30 percent chance of becoming infected. The chancres or sores of primary syphilis and the rashes and skin lesions of secondary syphilis are very infectious, so people with syphilis are most infectious during the primary and secondary stages of the infection, although the disease can be transmitted during certain later stages as well. The blood, semen, and vaginal secretions of an infected person may also be infectious.

Not only oral, anal, or genital sexual contact but even touching infected areas can result in transmission. People can transmit syphilis even if they are not symptomatic. Common routes through which the bacterium may enter the person being infected include breaks in the skin (which may be so tiny that they are invisible to the naked eye) or contact with mucous membranes.

## Testing for Syphilis

There are two ways in which syphilis is routinely diagnosed: (1) microscopic identification of the bacterium *Treponema pallidum* from swabs taken from the lesions and (2) identification of the body's immune response to the infection through the use of blood tests. Lesions that are moist, such as the chancres or skin lesions seen in secondary syphilis, can be swabbed and examined under a special microscope for the syphilis-causing bacterium. However, most clinics do not have the ability to perform this test or do not have clinicians who are expert at looking for the syphilis-causing bacterium in this way.

The syphilis blood tests are designed to detect antibodies, or proteins that the body makes in response to syphilis infection. The most common of these tests are the VDRL (Venereal Disease Research Laboratory) and RPR (rapid plasma reagin) tests. An infected person may take up to three months after infection to show up as positive, although most people do so within a few weeks of infection. These tests first show positive during primary syphilis, and they will remain positive (usually reaching a peak during secondary syphilis) unless a person receives treatment. If a person is successfully treated for syphilis, the tests will usually return to normal about twelve months after treatment. Thus, these two tests can be used to determine whether or not a given treatment for syphilis is effective.

A small percentage of the population (1–2%) will test positive on the VDRL and RPR tests even though they are not infected with syphilis. These false positive results are more common in pregnant women and in those who have an underlying medical problem (such as lupus) or another infection (such as tuberculosis).

If a person tests positive, then standard practice calls for a second test to be performed to determine whether or not he or she is really infected with syphilis. This second test, called the treponemal antibody test or fluorescent treponemal antibody absorbed test (FTA-ABS), is very specific for syphilis and is intended to detect different antibodies than the tests described earlier. This test occasionally also shows up positive in a person who is not infected with syphilis, but this result is rare. Once a person has a positive FTA-ABS test from infection with syphilis, this test rarely reverts back to normal, even after successful treatment; it is therefore not a good test for monitoring whether or not treatment has been successful.

These tests can also be performed on body fluids other than blood, such as fluid from the spinal canal to determine whether the infection is affecting the neurological system (neurosyphilis).

If all the tests for syphilis are negative and the disease is still suspected, a blood test is usually repeated at about three months from the suspected date of infection; as already noted, it may take up to three months after infection to show a positive blood test.

All partners within the last three months (or possibly within the last year, for those with later stages of the disease) of persons infected with syphilis should be screened. Those who have had sexual contact with a person who is thought to be infectious are usually treated despite negative test results. Anyone diagnosed with syphilis is usually evaluated for other sexually transmitted infections, since the likelihood of infection with other STDs is high. Infants with syphilis are tested in the same ways in which adults are. Syphilis is reportable to the health department in most states, and there are anonymous partner-notification programs, so that persons who may have been infected can be called in for treatment.

## The Treatment of Syphilis

The best treatment for syphilis is still one of the oldest antibiotics: penicillin. For the treatment of syphilis, penicillin must be given as an injection, not as an oral dose. The dosage and duration of treatment depend on the stage of the infection. For primary, secondary, and early latent syphilis, a single dose of penicillin usually eliminates the infection. Some people develop fever, chills, muscle aches, head-ache, and a worsening of the chancre or rash about eight hours after the shot; this reaction, called the *Jarisch-Herxheimer reaction*, is proba-bly due to the rapid killing of the bacteria. It is temporary, usually resolving within twenty-four hours, and it does not lead to perma-nent problems. It is not an allergic reaction to penicillin.

In a person who has late latent syphilis or syphilis of unknown duration, injections are given weekly for three consecutive weeks. A person who develops neurosyphilis must be hospitalized and receive intravenous penicillin for ten to fourteen days.

To determine if treatment has been successful, follow-up visits for a VDRL or RPR test are essential. If the treatment was successful, then the test result will be lower than it was previously. If treatment has not been successful, it may be because the infection has involved the nervous system; as already indicated, neurosyphilis is treatable but requires a longer course of therapy as well as hospitalization for the administration of intravenous antibiotics.

People who are allergic to penicillin may be treated with other medications, such as doxycycline and tetracycline, if they have pri-mary or secondary syphilis. However, in pregnant women the only recommended regimen is penicillin. The treatment may not be as effective in people infected with HIV as in those not infected, and for this reason close monitoring and follow-up testing are essential in HIV-positive persons.

The treatment for congenital syphilis (the infection of a newborn infant) must be coordinated with a specialist. The antibiotic used to treat children is also penicillin, and the course of treatment depends on the stage at which the child is diagnosed.

# THE GLOBAL HIV AND AIDS EPIDEMIC

Centers for Disease Control and Prevention

According to the Centers for Disease Control and Prevention (CDC), the human immunodeficiency virus (HIV) is the fourth leading cause of death worldwide. In the following selection, the CDC explains that in the United States and western Europe, the number of deaths from HIV and AIDS has decreased, but in sub-Saharan nations such as Botswana, where 36 percent of the adult population is infected with HIV, life expectancy has dropped ten years. The editors observe that HIV and AIDS seem to have had a greater impact on disadvantaged populations, which has made prevention and treatment efforts a challenge. The high costs of antiviral agents, for example, make it difficult for HIV-infected people in developing nations to receive needed treatment. The CDC is the leading federal agency for protecting the health and safety of people at home and abroad, providing credible information to enhance health decisions, and promoting health through strong partnerships.

Human immunodeficiency virus (HIV) infection and acquired immun-odeficiency syndrome (AIDS) are pandemic and pose one of the great-est challenges to global public health. As a bloodborne and sexually transmitted infection, HIV has variable patterns of transmission and impact among world regions and has disproportionately affected dis-advantaged or marginalized persons such as commercial sex workers, injection drug users, men who have sex with men (MSM), and persons living in poverty. HIV infection has caused approximately 20 million deaths; an estimated 36 million persons are infected. On the basis of data from the Joint United Nations Program on AIDS (UNAIDS) and other sources, this report summarizes epidemiologic trends, highlights several HIV and AIDS prevention milestones, and describes some pre-vention activities for the coming decade.

Sub-Saharan Africa (SSA) is the region of the world most severely affected by HIV and AIDS. Uganda, Kenya, and Tanzania were among

Excerpted from "The Global HIV and AIDS Epidemic, 2001," by the Centers for Disease Control and Prevention, *Morbidity and Mortality Weekly Report*, June 1, 2001.

the countries where the HIV epidemic was first recognized during the early 1980s. In 2000, an estimated 25.3 million persons in SSA were infected with HIV, and the average national prevalence of HIV infection among persons aged 15–49 years was 8.8%. Approximately four million new infections occurred during 2000. Approximately 10% of persons aged 15–49 years are infected in 16 countries, including seven in southern and eastern Africa, where approximately 20% are infected. In Botswana, the country with the highest prevalence, 36% of the adult population is infected with HIV.

Despite these trends, intensive and aggressive prevention programs for behavior change, condom promotion, voluntary HIV counseling and testing, and blood transfusion safety have lowered prevalence or slowed HIV transmission in several SSA countries. For example, in Uganda during 1990–2000, overall adult HIV prevalence declined from 14% to 8%. In Masaka, Uganda, HIV prevalence among females aged 20–24 years decreased from 20.9% during 1989–1990 to 13.8% during 1996–1997. Also, in Lusaka, Zambia, which had an early and severe epidemic, HIV prevalence declined among females aged 15–19 years attending prenatal clinics from 27% in 1993 to 17% in 1998. In West Africa, Senegal has maintained a prevalence of approximately 2%; prevention efforts have included regulating commercial sex, intensive condom promotion, treatment of sexually transmitted diseases (STDs), and community mobilization.

The epidemic continues to spread in the world's most populous areas, where the infrastructure for an effective response is underdeveloped. In China, HIV prevalence was as high as 82% among injection drug users and 6% in commercial sex workers during 1998–1999. A sustained increase also occurred in all reported STDs among males and females during 1989–1998. In India, the estimated HIV infection rate among persons aged 15–49 years is 0.7%. As of mid-1998, an estimated 3.5 million persons were infected with HIV. An exception to countries with increasing prevalence is Thailand, where the epidemic began in the mid-1980s among injection drug users and commercial sex workers and their clients and spread rapidly to the wider population through heterosexual transmission. In response, health officials developed HIV and AIDS surveillance systems and mounted a sustained and effective response, including the "100% condom use" campaign for commercial sex. The resulting decline in STD and HIV transmission was reflected in a decrease in STD rates and HIV prevalence in military recruits and women attending prenatal clinics.

Eastern Europe has had recent and rapid growth of HIV infection among injection drug users. By January 1999, approximately 10,000 HIV cases had been reported in the Russian Federation. By December 2000, the cumulative total increased to 70,000, and HIV infection among injection drug users was reported from 82 of the 89 regions in the Russian Federation. Ukraine was the country most affected in Eastern Europe and Central Asia, where newly reported infections increased from 47 cases per year during 1992–1994 to approximately 15,000 cases in 1997. Ukraine accounted for 90% of all AIDS cases reported in the region in 1998 and 1999. HIV probably will spread further in the region as a result of the large number of injection drug users, increasing rates of STDs, the growing commercial sex industry, and socioeconomic transitions.

In Western Europe and the United States, deaths attributed to HIV have declined substantially since the introduction of highly active antiretroviral therapies. However, reported increases in STDs among MSM and other indicators of increased risk-taking behavior may be leading to an increase in HIV transmission.

In Latin America and the Caribbean, the leading modes of transmission include sex between men, sex between men and women, and injection drug use. By December 2000, an estimated 1.4 million adults and children were infected with HIV/AIDS in the region compared with 1.3 million in 1999. Barbados, Belize, Dominican Republic, Guyana, Haiti, and Suriname have an HIV prevalence of approximately 1%. The Caribbean, with an adult prevalence of 2.1%, is the second most affected world region. In Brazil, reported HIV-related deaths have declined from approximately 25 per 100,000 in 1995 to approximately 15 per 100,000 in 1999, in large part because of the government policy of providing universal, free access to antiretroviral therapies.

HIV and AIDS is the leading cause of death in Africa and the fourth leading cause of death worldwide. In the countries most affected in Africa, life expectancy has declined by 10 years and infant death rates have doubled. In countries with the highest prevalence, such as Botswana, South Africa, and Zimbabwe, the full impact of the epidemic has not been felt because those infected recently have not developed symptoms. Equally important is the effect of HIV deaths on families, social systems, and national growth and development. Young adults who contribute substantially to countries' gross domestic product are most commonly affected. In families, loss of one or both parents to HIV can lead to loss of income, cessation of children's education, increased child labor, and disruption of family and social support systems. For example, in Zambia, a shortage of school teachers has occurred because more teachers are dying of AIDS than can be trained to replace them.

## The Challenges of Prevention

Considerable heterogeneity of rates exist in HIV-infected countries throughout the world, and the differences have been attributed to risk factors associated with the spread of HIV and AIDS. They include migration, economic instability, drug use, STDs, low levels of literacy, and poverty. These are formidable challenges to implementing effective prevention programs. Although the earliest epidemiologic studies described the modes of transmission of HIV and AIDS and provided insights into the types of interventions needed to prevent transmission, this understanding has been difficult to translate into effective interventions worldwide. The HIV epidemic has challenged public health agencies to develop new and often controversial prevention programs that contradict established practices and social norms.

Despite these challenges, even countries with modest resources have demonstrated that the epidemic can be stabilized or reversed. In these countries, successful programs have included strong, high-level political leadership for HIV prevention, a national program plan, adequate funding, and strong community involvement. Effective and feasible interventions for HIV prevention and control are available. Quality testing and guidelines for blood use can promote a safer blood supply. Widespread condom promotion can reduce HIV seroprevalance in high-risk populations, and education programs for young persons can result in decreased risk-taking behavior. Increasing access to drug treatment and providing education about and increasing access to clean syringes can reduce infection risk in drug using populations. Prophylaxis with co-trimoxazole can prevent certain opportunistic infections and reduce the number of HIV-related deaths. Administering antiviral agents, such as niverapine or short-course zidovudine, and advice to women on breastfeeding, can substantially reduce mother-to-infant transmission. Improving treatment for STDs can slow HIV infection rates. When effective STD treatment programs continue to be compromised by weak infrastructure, important opportunities for HIV prevention are lost. Efforts are needed to strengthen STD services and to integrate these with HIV prevention and control programs.

The social stigma associated with HIV infection in many cultures combined with difficulties in providing treatment or services for infected persons are major barriers to expanding voluntary counseling and testing for HIV. Persons who may benefit from knowing their serostatus often reject counseling and testing because they fear the consequences of disclosure of their HIV status. Other disincentives are the lack of resources for care and treatment and the sense that little is gained from learning that one is infected with HIV. Prevention programs must be accompanied by efforts to improve the care of HIV-infected persons. Isoniazid prophylaxis for TB and other low-cost interventions should be incorporated into prevention programs.

The most effective intervention therapy for persons infected with HIV is the use of a combination of antiretroviral agents. However, the high cost of these regimens and the infrastructure needed to monitor their use have put these medications beyond the reach of most HIV-infected persons. Although the price of these drugs has fallen, making treatment a possibility for a greater number of persons, infrastructures to support the effective use of these medications remain inadequate and need strengthening. Given the needs for both prevention and treatment, public health officials and international donors will need to determine the best mix of drug treatment and prevention programs.

Globally, the HIV epidemic has intersected with other, underlying public health problems, most notably tuberculosis (TB). TB remains the principal cause of death in persons with HIV infection worldwide. National TB rates have escalated over the past decade in SSA and South-East Asia. Since the mid-1980s, in many African countries with well-organized programs, annual TB notification rates have increased fourfold, reaching peaks of more than 400 cases per 100,000 population. In some countries, up to 70% of patients with sputum smear-positive pulmonary TB are HIV-infected. To the extent possible, integration of HIV and TB prevention programs should be a priority in these countries.

The increase in HIV infection and AIDS deaths has led to increases in aid from governments and national and international organizations and foundations. Since 1999, the U.S. government increased its financial support to HIV/AIDS prevention and care programs in affected countries. For fiscal year 2001, this totaled $457.5 million. Participating agencies include the U.S. Agency for International Development, the U.S. Department of Health and Human Services (including CDC, and the Health Resources and Services Administration), the Department of Defense, the Department of Labor, and the Department of Commerce. The National Institutes of Health recently launched the Comprehensive International Program for Research on AIDS (CIPRA) to assist developing countries with research agendas relevant to their populations and to enhance infrastructure. CDC established the Global AIDS Program (GAP) to implement international HIV prevention efforts in collaboration with other federal agencies. The program emphasizes sustaining intervention programs for primary prevention of HIV infection, infrastructure development and laboratory support, and home- and community-based care for persons with HIV infection. CDC is supporting these activities in 24 countries in partnership with other U.S. agencies, national ministries of health, UNAIDS, and other international agencies.

# THE RELATIONSHIP BETWEEN HUMAN PAPILLOMAVIRUSES AND CANCER

National Cancer Institute

*In the following selection, the National Cancer Institute identifies human papillomavirus (HPV) infection as one of the most common sexually transmitted diseases and a primary cause of cervical cancer. According to the institute, researchers postulate that HPVs produce proteins that can interfere with the cell functions that normally prevent excessive growth, or cancer. To determine the chance of contracting HPV, the institute identifies risk factors, including having multiple partners and beginning to have sex in the teen years. Although HPV is incurable, early detection can provide women and their doctors with more treatment options, the institute claims. The National Cancer Institute is a component of the National Institutes of Health, one of eight agencies that compose the Public Health Service in the Department of Health and Human Services.*

Human papillomaviruses (HPVs) are a group of more than 100 types of viruses. They are called papillomaviruses because certain types may cause warts, or papillomas, which are benign (noncancerous) tumors. The HPVs that cause the common warts which grow on hands and feet are different from those that cause growths in the mouth and genital area. Some types of HPVs are associated with certain types of cancer.

Of the more than 100 types of HPVs, over 30 types can be passed from one person to another through sexual contact. HPV infection is one of the most common sexually transmitted diseases (STDs). Some types of HPVs may cause warts to appear on or around the genitals or anus. Genital warts (technically known as condylomata acuminatum) are most commonly associated with two HPV types, numbers 6 and 11. Warts may appear within several weeks after sexual contact with a person who has HPV, or they may take months or years to appear; or they may never appear. HPVs may also cause flat, abnormal growths in the genital area and on the cervix (the lower part of the uterus that extends into the vagina). HPV infections often do not cause any symptoms.

## The Cancer Link

HPVs are now recognized as the major cause of cervical cancer. Studies also suggest that HPVs may play a role in cancers of the anus, vulva, vagina, and penis, and some cancers of the oropharynx (the middle part of the throat that includes the soft palate, the base of the tongue, and the tonsils).

Some types of HPVs are referred to as "low-risk" viruses because they rarely develop into cancer; these include HPV-6 and HPV-11. HPV viruses that can lead to the development of cancer are referred to as "high-risk." Both high-risk and low-risk types of HPVs can cause the growth of abnormal cells, but generally only the high-risk types of HPVs may lead to cancer. Sexually transmitted, high-risk HPVs have been linked with cancer in both men and women; they include HPV types 16, 18, 31, 33, 35, 39, 45, 51, 52, 56, 58, 59, 68, and 69. These high-risk types of HPVs cause growths that are usually flat and nearly invisible, as compared with the warts caused by HPV-6 and HPV-11. It is important to note, however, that the majority of HPV infections go away on their own and do not cause any abnormal growths.

Abnormal cervical cells can be detected when a Pap test is done during a gynecologic exam. Various terms have been used to describe the abnormal cells that may be seen in Pap tests. In the Bethesda system (the major system used to report the results of Pap tests in the United States), precancerous conditions are divided into low-grade and high-grade squamous intraepithelial lesions (SILs). Squamous cells are thin, flat cells that cover internal and external surfaces of the body, including the tissue that forms the surface of the skin, the lining of the hollow organs of the body, and the passages of the genital, respiratory, and digestive tracts. Other terms sometimes used to describe these abnormal cells are cervical intraepithelial neoplasia (CIN) and dysplasia. Low-grade SILs (mild dysplasias) are a common condition, especially in young women. The majority of low-grade SILs return to normal over months to a few years. Sometimes, low-grade SILs can progress to high-grade SILs. High-grade SILs are not cancer, but they may eventually lead to cancer and should be treated by a doctor.

Behaviors such as beginning sexual intercourse at an early age (especially age 16 or younger) and having many sexual partners increase the chance that a woman will develop an HPV infection in the cervix. Most HPV infections go away on their own without causing any type of abnormality. It is important to note that infection with high-risk HPV types may increase the chance that mild abnormalities will progress to more severe abnormalities or cervical cancer. Still, of the women who do develop abnormal cell changes with high-risk types of HPV, only a small percentage will develop cervical cancer if the abnormal cells are not removed. Studies suggest that whether a woman develops cervical cancer depends on a variety of factors acting together with high-risk HPVs. The factors that may increase the risk of cancer in women with HPV infection include smoking, having many children, and human immunodeficiency virus (HIV) infection.

## Preventing and Treating HPV

Screening for cervical cancer consists of regular Pap tests for women who are sexually active or who have reached 18 years of age. If high-grade abnormal cell changes are found on a Pap test, colposcopy and biopsy of any abnormal areas are recommended. (Colposcopy is a procedure in which a lighted magnifying instrument called a colposcope is used to examine the vagina and cervix. Biopsy is the removal of a small piece of tissue for diagnosis.) If low-grade changes are found, repeat Pap tests or colposcopy may be recommended.

Although there is currently no medical cure to eliminate a papillomavirus infection, the SILs and warts these viruses cause can be treated. Methods used to treat SILs include cryosurgery (freezing that destroys tissue), laser treatment (surgery using a high-intensity light), LEEP (loop electrosurgical excision procedure, the removal of tissue using a hot wire loop), as well as conventional surgery. Similar treatments may be used for external genital warts. In addition, three powerful chemicals (podophyllin, bichloroacetic acid, and trichloroacetic acid) will destroy external genital warts when applied directly to them. Podofilox (podophyllotoxin) can be applied topically either as a liquid or a gel to external genital warts. Imiquimod cream has also been approved to treat external warts. Also, fluorouracil cream (sometimes called 5-FU) may be used to treat the warts. Some doctors use interferon alpha to treat warts that have recurred after being removed by traditional means. Imiquimod and interferon alpha work by stimulating the immune (defense) system to fight the virus.

The ASCUS/LSIL Triage Study (ALTS), a major study organized and funded by the National Cancer Institute (NCI), is currently evaluating different management approaches for women with mildly abnormal Pap test results. (ASCUS and LSIL are acronyms for the two mild abnormalities detected by Pap tests. ASCUS stands for atypical squamous cells of undetermined significance and LSIL for low-grade squamous intraepithelial lesions.) Preliminary findings from the ALTS study suggest that testing cervical samples for HPV is an excellent option to help direct followup for women with an ASCUS Pap test result. Repeat Pap tests or direct referral to colposcopy remain options for the followup of ASCUS results. The final study results, which are expected to be published in 2004, will help women and their doctors decide what course of action to take when mild abnormalities show up on Pap tests.

Researchers at NCI and elsewhere are studying how HPVs cause precancerous changes in normal cells and how these changes can be prevented. They are using HPVs grown in the laboratory to find ways to prevent the infection and its associated disease and to create vaccines against the viruses. Vaccines for certain papillomaviruses, such as HPV-16 and HPV-18, are being studied in clinical trials (research studies with people) for cervical cancer; similar trials for other types of cancer are planned.

Laboratory research has indicated that HPVs produce proteins known as E5, E6, and E7. These proteins interfere with the cell functions that normally prevent excessive growth. For example, HPV E6 interferes with the human protein p53. p53 is present in all people and acts to keep tumors from growing. This research is being used to develop ways to interrupt the process by which HPV infection can lead to growth of abnormal cells and, eventually, cancer.

CHAPTER 2

# THE IMPACT OF
# SEXUALLY TRANSMITTED
# DISEASES

Contemporary Issues
Companion

# THE IMPACT OF SEXUALLY TRANSMITTED DISEASES: AN OVERVIEW

American Social Health Association

In the following selection, a panel of researchers from the American Social Health Association (ASHA) discuss the scope and impact of sexually transmitted diseases (STDs). The panel's research reveals that STDs are among the most common infections in the United States. In addition, the panel explains that some populations are at greater risk than others. They observe, for example, that women are more vulnerable to STDs than men. According to the authors, not only are the direct and indirect medical costs associated with the treatment of STDs extremely high, STDs also have a high cost in terms of pain, suffering, and grief. ASHA is a private organization whose goal is to stop the transmission of STDs and their tragic consequences.

Sexually transmitted diseases (STDs) are among the most common infections in the United States. In 1996 one STD—chlamydia—was the most frequently reported infectious disease in the country, according to the Centers for Disease Control and Prevention (CDC). Of the top 10 most frequently reported infections, five are STDs. Most Americans are unaware of the extent of the STD epidemic, however, because many infections are asymptomatic, and because social stigma prevents open discussion of the topic.

The silent nature of the STD epidemic is perhaps its greatest public health threat, as people continue to underestimate their risk or forgo testing because they have no symptoms. In addition, a potentially deadly aspect of STDs is the link to HIV. STD infections increase susceptibility to acquiring HIV, the virus that causes AIDS. Clearly the continued spread of STDs is costly in terms of both health care dollars and human suffering. However, many effective treatments and prevention strategies exist that can help stop the STD epidemic if we understand who is affected and the cost-effectiveness of prevention.

Excerpted from *Sexually Transmitted Diseases in America: How Many Cases and at What Cost?* by the American Social Health Association (Research Triangle Park, NC: American Social Health Association, 2001). Copyright © 2001 by the American Social Health Association. Reprinted with permission.

## Who Is Affected?

Americans of every age and every geographic, racial, cultural, socio-economic, and religious background are affected by STDs. Infections such as herpes and HPV are so prevalent that almost everyone is at risk, and many are already infected.

More than half of teens ages 15–19 have had sex, and these teens are at high risk for STDs. About a quarter of all new cases of STDs occur in teens; two-thirds of cases occur in people ages 15–24. By age 24, at least one in three sexually active people will have contracted an STD. Why are young people at such great risk? They are more likely to be single, have multiple sex partners and to engage in other risky behaviors than older people. In addition, teenage girls are highly susceptible to contracting chlamydia and gonorrhea, because these diseases easily infect the immature cervix.

Biologically and socially, women are more vulnerable than men to STDs. Genital infections including HIV are more easily passed from men to women than from women to men. Women are less likely to have noticeable symptoms unless complications occur. They are then more likely to experience long-term consequences such as infertility, tubal pregnancy and cervical cancer. Many women face obstacles protecting themselves from STDs: in general, women have less say than men over whether to have sex, and whether condoms are used.

Virtually every STD can be passed from a pregnant woman to her fetus or infant, often with tragic consequences. Because infants' immune systems are still developing, infections that are serious for an adult can be life-threatening for an infant. Common STD-related problems for infants include low birth weight, premature birth, conjunctivitis, pneumonia, neurologic problems, and congenital abnormalities.

Other groups disproportionately affected by STDs include people who are poor, lack access to health care, and are geographically isolated, including ethnic minorities, who often fall into all these groups. Within the United States, some STDs—particularly gonorrhea, chlamydia, syphilis and HIV—tend to be highest in Southern states. Overall, however, STD rates do not vary greatly by region.

## What Is Being Done?

Several strategies have proven effective at lowering rates of STDs in the United States. Most notably, CDC and state and local programs for the control of chlamydia, gonorrhea and syphilis have dramatically reduced the numbers of these infections. Education and counseling programs have changed sexual behaviors in some high-risk communities. In addition, new diagnostic techniques are helping health care providers find and treat many asymptomatic infections. New, single-dose treatments are available to cure bacterial STDs and provide safe options for treating pregnant women. National media have also played a key role in educating the public about STD prevalence and risk.

Despite these advances in treatment and prevention, however, the United States continues to have the highest STD rates of any country in the industrialized world. No effective national program for STD prevention exists, and state programs vary widely in funding and impact. The American public remains generally unaware of the risk for STDs and the importance of prevention and screening.

A 1998 Kaiser Family Foundation/*Glamour* magazine survey found that most men and women of reproductive age (18–44 years old) seriously underestimate how common STDs are and their personal risk for getting an STD. While an estimated one in four Americans will get an STD in their lifetime, the majority of men (74%) and women (69%) think the rate is one in ten Americans or fewer. Only 14 percent of all men and 8 percent of all women say they think they are at risk for STDs—and single men and women are not much more likely to feel they are at risk. Perhaps for this reason, condom use is far from consistent among many couples; two-thirds of single men and women say they do not "always" use condoms. The story is similar among teens 15–17 years: the majority of teen girls (73%) and boys (77%) think the STD rate is one in ten Americans or fewer in a lifetime. Only one in five teens say they think they are at risk of getting an STD.

The secrecy and shame surrounding STDs interfere with communication between parents and children, sexual partners, teachers and students, and even patients and health care providers. In a Gallop Organization poll commissioned by the American Social Health Association (ASHA) in 1995, over half of adults and over one-third of teens said their health care providers spend "no time at all" discussing STDs with them. Another Kaiser Family Foundation/*Glamour* survey conducted in 1997 found that STDs are rarely discussed during OB/GYN visits, and that providers may not be asking adequate risk-assessment questions. As greater numbers of Americans receive their health care through managed care organizations, it will be critical for these and other private health care providers to take the initiative in counseling, screening, diagnosing and treating patients for STDs. Teenagers, in particular, need and deserve better information, counseling and access to health care.

There is a clear need for public and private sector organizations, medical professionals, educational systems, the media, and religious and community groups to break the silence on the topic of sexual health. Public education programs are essential to alert consumers, health care providers and policy makers to the reality of the STD epidemic. The mass media can be extremely powerful in promoting healthy behaviors and balanced sexual messages.

Clearly, more progress is needed and is feasible. With the currently available testing and treatment technologies, the United States has never had better tools for addressing its large and costly STD epidemic.

Effective prevention to reduce the spread of STDs now can prevent
both growing health care costs and continued human suffering. . . .

## The Prevalence of STDs

STDs remain a major public health problem in the United States. However, estimating the overall incidence and prevalence of STDs is a complex and elusive task. Until the release of this report in December 1998,
the most widely quoted figure has been 12 million sexually transmitted
infections occurring annually. The scientific basis for this number has
not been closely examined, and variants have been proposed. For
example, for 1994, the sum of the specific STDs listed in the Institute of
Medicine's report was 10.5 million new cases annually, while a 1998
NIH Program Announcement cited 14 million STDs annually.

Are 12 million cases of STDs an accurate estimate of STDs for the
United States in 1998? Several developments suggest a readjustment is
in order. Because control programs directed against gonorrhea and
syphilis have enjoyed successes, the incidence and prevalence of these
infections have declined. Chlamydia control programs, which have
emphasized increased screening, have led to a paradoxical (though
predictable) situation where reported cases are increasing despite
decreasing incidence and prevalence. Also, improved detection techniques have made us aware of the unrecognized extent of genital herpes, human papillomavirus, and trichomoniasis. This review examines the available published evidence to provide an updated point
estimate and range for the incidence and prevalence of selected STDs
in the United States. . . .

In the United States, the incidence of reported genital chlamydial
infections and viral STDs steadily increased in the late 1990s, while
the incidence of gonorrhea generally declined during the same interval. However, the actual number of chlamydial infections probably
fell as control programs expanded. Levels of syphilis varied among
different population subgroups, but have reached record lows since
1995. Vaginal infections such as trichomonas and bacterial vaginosis
have probably remained high, although surveillance for these conditions is rudimentary.

## The Prevalence of Curable, Bacterial STDs

Genital chlamydial infections became the most prevalent bacterial
STD in the United States during the 1980s, at the time gonorrhea levels began declining. In 1996, nearly 500,000 cases of genital chlamydia were reported to CDC, exceeding all other notifiable diseases in
the United States. Reported chlamydial infections in women greatly
exceed those in men, primarily because screening programs have been
directed to that group. Moreover, chlamydial prevalence is strongly
correlated with younger age and heterosexual behaviors. A previous
estimate of 4 million new chlamydial infections annually in the

United States was made in 1986, using a prevalence ratio approach. Because the expansion of chlamydia control programs has probably led to declining chlamydial prevalence in the interim, this estimate has been updated. In 1997, between 2.6 and 3.2 million new cases of genital chlamydia were estimated to have occurred in persons aged 10–44 years. As a point estimate, we chose 3 million new chlamydia infections having occurred in 1996.

Gonorrhea trends have been quite consistent ever since 1975. The number of reported gonorrhea cases has generally declined, starting in the mid-1970s with the introduction of the national gonorrhea control program. A disproportionate share of the decline occurred among older, white populations, with infection rates remaining relatively high among minority races and adolescents. In addition, reported gonorrhea is associated with a younger mean age than syphilis among all gender and race categories. In 1996, CDC reported 325,900 new cases of gonorrhea. Because previous investigations have shown about half of all diagnosed gonorrhea cases are reported to public health authorities, an estimated total of 650,000 new gonorrhea infections occurred in 1996.

Syphilis trends have followed a roller coaster course for the last half-century. Its incidence rose during World War II, but fell thereafter, coinciding with the introduction of penicillin. The lowest levels were observed at the end of the 1950s, but from the 1960s on, the incidence of syphilis increased. A rapidly rising male-to-female ratio coincided with the spread of syphilis among men having sex with men throughout the 1970s. However, in the 1980s, indicative of the safer sexual behaviors stimulated by HIV prevention messages, syphilis cases in gay males declined precipitously. This encouraging trend was directly countered by the number of climbing syphilis cases during the late 1980s among heterosexuals of minority races, in large part fueled by the crack epidemic. Nonetheless, during the 1990s, syphilis levels again fell to numbers seen two decades earlier, leading public health authorities to entertain notions of syphilis elimination. In 1996, CDC reported 11,400 new cases of primary and secondary syphilis and 53,000 new cases of all stages of syphilis. Accounting for an estimated 20% underreporting, approximately 70,000 total syphilis infections in 1996 were estimated to have been diagnosed.

## The Prevalence of Incurable, Viral STDs

The numbers of symptomatic genital herpes cases increased eleven fold during the 1970s and 1980s. Genital herpes causes at least ten times more genital ulcer cases than does syphilis. A comprehensive analysis of existing national databases estimated nearly 150,000 clinical visits for genital herpes in 1992. Moreover, investigations have shown that symptomatic infections caused by herpes simplex viruses (HSV) are only the tip of the iceberg. Infection with HSV-2 has occurred among an estimated 45 million Americans, even though less than one-quarter perceive themselves ever to have had genital herpes. Based on differences between HSV-2 levels measured cross-sectionally in the late 1970s and the late 1980s, up to 1 million new HSV-2 infections may be transmitted each year in the United States. This number ignores the sizable percentage of genital herpes contributed by HSV-1, and thus might be considered a minimum estimate.

Likewise, the diagnosis of symptomatic genital warts caused by the human papilloma viruses (HPV) has been skyrocketing since the late 1970s. Its asymptomatic counterparts, HPV infections of the cervix and vagina, have emerged as the most common STD among sexually active young populations. The cumulative three-year incidence of HPV infection among college-aged students was 43 percent, with a duration of eight months. Using conservative assumptions and extrapolating these data to the general U.S. population, one obtains an annual estimate of at least 5.5 million new HPV infections each year. Likewise, a conservative estimate of the prevalence of productive HPV (that is, persons with active shedding of HPV DNA) is approximately 20 million.

Hepatitis B, despite the availability of a preventive vaccine, still remains among the main sexually transmitted viral infections. Approximately two-thirds of the total incident hepatitis B cases are spread sexually. Based on CDC estimates of 128,000 overall HBV infections in the U.S. in 1995, we count 77,000 incident sexually transmitted hepatitis B cases. Based on serological measures from the third National Health and Nutrition Examination Survey, NHANES-III, an estimated total of 1,250,000 prevalent cases of chronic hepatitis B exist in the United States. Thus, we estimate a prevalence of approximately 750,000 currently infectious persons with sexually acquired HBV. . . .

HIV infection epidemic trends in the U.S. have been evolving. Beginning in the mid-1970s, HIV was transmitted primarily among homosexual and bisexual men, and AIDS was first diagnosed in this group by the early to mid-1980s. The virus entered the injection drug-using (IDU) populations in the early 1980s and rapidly spread during the decade. Limited heterosexual transmission occurred until the late 1980s. However, since 1989, the greatest proportionate increase of reported AIDS cases has been among heterosexuals, and this trend is expected to continue. In 1993, an estimated 750,000 persons in the U.S. were infected with HIV, with approximately 40,000 new infections occurring each year. By 1996, another approach to estimating HIV incidence and prevalence yielded an estimate of 41,000 new HIV infections annually, with between 700,000 to 800,000 prevalent HIV infections. The introduction of protease inhibitors may increase the number of prevalent infections by extending the life of HIV-infected people. Approximately half of the incident and three-quarters of prevalent infections were estimated to have been sexually transmitted. Thus, it appears as if the incidence of HIV has been relatively stable during the late 1990s. Globally, the incidence of HIV is much higher, with an estimated 5.8 million new HIV infections annually and more than 30 million persons currently living with HIV. More than 90% of the global total has been spread sexually. . . .

## The Cost of STDs

The ASHA panel reviewed published data on the economic costs of individual STDs and estimated the direct medical costs of STD treatment for all estimated cases per year. Direct medical costs are dollars actually spent within the health care system treating STDs and their complications. The direct costs presented here—$8.4 billion—are only one part of the total economic burden of the STD epidemic. These estimates do not include nonmedical indirect costs (lost wages and productivity due to STD-related illness), out-of-pocket costs, or the costs incurred when STDs are transmitted to infants, which can result in significant lifelong expenditures. In addition, many STD cases result in an office visit but are not diagnosed as STDs. Finally, these estimates do not include the cost of STD prevention and screening.

It is useful to look at the costs for treating bacterial and viral STDs separately, because the nature of these infections is quite different. Treatment of bacterial STDs most often results in a cure; the course of therapy is limited and relatively inexpensive. By far the greatest costs associated with bacterial STDs result from complications of untreated chlamydia and gonorrhea, which can lead to pelvic inflammatory disease (PID). Viral STDs, in contrast, cannot be cured and may require treatment over a period of years. The greatest costs associated with viral STDs result from treatment of precancerous cervical lesions caused by HPV infection, and treatment of sexually transmitted HIV/AIDS.

In addition to the economic impact of STDs, the panel noted that STDs have a high human cost in terms of pain, suffering and grief. Complications of chlamydia and gonorrhea can lead to chronic pain, infertility and tubal pregnancies, which can affect a woman's health and well-being throughout her lifetime. The harmful impact of STDs on infants leads to long-term emotional suffering and stress for families, which cannot be captured in dollar terms. Unlike other diseases, STDs often cause stigma and feelings of shame for patients diagnosed with these infections. According to a 1998 Kaiser Family Foundation/ *Glamour* survey of adults, almost half of men (44%) and women (47%) say if they were in a new relationship and discovered their partner had an STD, they would be "a lot less likely" to continue the relationship, with another third saying they would be "somewhat less likely" (30% men, 29% women). Most say they would feel "angry" at the person they got it from if they found out they had an STD, though women (87%) are more likely than men (74%) to say so.

# Underestimating the Risk of STDs

The Henry J. Kaiser Family Foundation

A survey conducted by the Henry J. Kaiser Family Foundation and *Glamour* magazine reveals how little Americans know about sexually transmitted diseases (STDs). In the following selection, the foundation explains that many Americans are unaware of some of the most harmful STDs and underestimate their risk of contracting these diseases. The authors reveal, for example, that only 8 percent of women believed themselves to be at risk of contracting an STD when in fact, research reveals that one in four Americans will get an STD in their lifetime. Moreover, the authors write, although most believe that those with STDs have the responsibility to reveal this information to their partners, in practice fear of being stigmatized often inhibits them from doing so. The Henry J. Kaiser Family Foundation is a philanthropy that focuses on major health care issues facing the nation.

There is a dramatic difference between the way people think things should be and how they really are when it comes to STDs: men and women say that they would feel comfortable talking about STDs with their sexual partner, but in reality, only half have had such conversations. Almost all men and women think people should tell their sexual partner if they have an STD, but men and women who have had an STD struggle with telling their partners, and often tell them *after* the fact, if at all. Americans may find it difficult to be as open about STDs as they want to be in part because of the stigma STDs still carry: most men and women say they would probably stop dating a sexual partner if they found out he or she had an STD, and half of those who have had an STD say having one has made them feel "ashamed" or "embarrassed."

## A Gap in Knowledge

Eighty-five percent of women and 83 percent of men say they know a "fair" amount or "a lot" about STDs—but there are crucial gaps in their knowledge.

When asked to name STDs they have heard of, very few men or

women know of the most common, and potentially damaging, STDs. More than half of men and women mention gonorrhea and syphilis, while only 34 percent of women and 22 percent of men name chlamydia—the most common bacterial STD in women, which when left untreated, can develop into pelvic inflammatory disease (PID), the leading preventable cause of infertility in the U.S. Even fewer women (13%) and men (8%) name genital warts or human papillomavirus (HPV), the virus that causes them. New research shows that HPV may be the most common of all STDs, present in an estimated one-quarter to three-quarters of all men and women of reproductive age.

Not knowing the names of specific diseases indicates a larger problem, according to Felicia H. Stewart, M.D., Director of Reproductive Health Programs at Kaiser Family Foundation: "You can't talk to your doctor or partner about something you don't even know exists."

More women (81%) than men (68%) are aware that women can experience long-term health problems, such as infertility or cervical cancer, from having an STD. A minority of women (33%) or men (24%) are aware that a *woman* is more likely to get an STD from an infected *man* than vice versa.

Despite some general knowledge of STDs, very few men or women have an accurate picture of how prevalent STDs are in this country. Whereas the Centers for Disease Control and Prevention estimate that at least one in four Americans will get an STD at some point in their lifetime, the majority of men (74%) and women (69%) think the rate is one in ten Americans or fewer.

Perhaps because people dramatically underestimate the size of this "hidden epidemic," only a handful of men and women feel they are *personally* at risk of getting an STD. Only 14 percent of all men and 8 percent of all women say they think they are at risk of getting one—and single men (24%) and women (15%) are not much more likely to feel they are at risk. Maybe because they do not believe themselves to be at risk, condom use is far from consistent among many couples: two-thirds of single men and women say they do not "always" use condoms.

Perhaps also as a result of not believing they are at risk, few women—and even fewer men—are getting tested for STDs. Sixty-one percent of men and 48 percent of women have never been tested for an STD other than HIV/AIDS. Of those who have been tested, men are especially likely to say they were tested because they had symptoms (22%)—which implies they were already infected and infectious at that time. Furthermore, some men who think they were tested may be wrong. "Men think if they donate blood or have a blood test for another procedure that they will be tested for all STDs; that is simply not true," says Dr. Stewart. "In fact, STDs aren't even being discussed as part of routine counseling for these men. Less than half of the men say they have ever talked with a health professional about STDs."

## Are People Honest About Their STDs?

Virtually all men and women agree that people have "a great deal of responsibility" to tell their sexual partners if they are infected with an STD (97% women, 96% men). And when it comes to their own situation, many men and women say they would feel comfortable discussing the topic of STDs with a sexual partner (66% women, 59% men).

Those who have had an STD say it is much harder to tell their partners than most men and women think it would be. In practice, only about a third of men and women who said they have had an STD say they revealed that fact to their current or most recent partner *before* they had sexual intercourse (34% women, 28% men). And even though two-thirds of all men and women say they would feel "comfortable" talking about STDs with a partner, only half have actually had such a conversation with their current or most recent partner (56% women, 51% men)—and only half of *them* talked before having sexual intercourse.

"There's a yawning gap between theory and practice on STDs: young men and women are talking the talk, but they are not walking the walk in terms of condom use, STD conversations, and getting tested," says Cynthia Leive, Senior Editor, News and Features, *Glamour*.

Few may be able to discuss STDs in part because these infections still carry a stigma for many people. Half of the men and women who said they have had an STD say having one has made them feel "ashamed or embarrassed." Almost half of all men (44%) and women (47%) say if they were in a new relationship and discovered their partner had an STD, they would be "a lot less likely" to continue the relationship, with another third saying they would be "somewhat less likely" (30% men, 29% women). Most say they would feel "angry" at the person they got it from if they found out *they* had an STD, though women (87%) are more likely than men to say so (74%).

# THE ECONOMIC PRICE OF STDS

David Anderson

In the following selection, David Anderson explains that prompt treatment of bacterial STDs such as chlamydia and gonorrhea involves minimal cost, but the longer those diseases go untreated, the more expensive the treatment will be. These diseases are the leading cause of pelvic inflammatory disease (PID), which can result in dangerous ectopic pregnancies, even infertility. According to the author, broader screening practices and partner notification may reduce the number of STD cases and, ultimately, lower their costs in terms of health care and human suffering. Anderson is editor of *NIDA Notes*, a publication of the National Institute on Drug Abuse, and a contributing editor for *Business & Health*.

Early detection of STDs can drastically reduce treatment cost and human suffering, but health plans won't find these cases unless they look for them.

Love may be free, but the price tag for sexually transmitted disease (STD) is steep indeed. Twenty-five STDs cost the United States $10 billion in 1995, according to the National Center for HIV, STD and TB Prevention (NCHSTP), a branch of the Centers for Disease Control and Prevention. And that does not include AIDS or HIV, the virus that causes it.

Chlamydia, gonorrhea, syphilis, human papillomavirus infection, genital herpes and hepatitis A and B are the significant non-HIV STDs in terms of morbidity, mortality and cost. HIV will not be discussed here—except to note that having any other STD raises the risk for it and that it added another $7 billion to that 1995 tally.

## The Price of Bacterial STDs

Chlamydia infected an estimated 4 million Americans in 1995, making it the most common STD. . . . Chlamydia is a leading cause of pelvic inflammatory disease (PID), which costs around $19,000 if it is treated in a hospital. PID in turn is responsible for half of all ectopic pregnancies and a large portion of tubal blockage leading to infertility.

Excerpted from "The Price of Pleasure," by David Anderson, *Business & Health*, April 1998. Copyright © 1998 by Thomson Medical Economics. Reprinted with permission.

While men with chlamydia generally develop irritation or penile discharge, women, who are liable to the disease's devastating and life-threatening complications, often have no symptoms. The NCHSTP advises screening women for chlamydia if their age, number of sexual partners and other characteristics place them at elevated risk. A recent study at a family planning clinic demonstrated that a more aggressive approach—screening every woman under age 30—uncovered 25 percent more cases at roughly the same average cost per case: $3,500 compared to $3,600.

Group Health of Puget Sound in Washington credits screening with reducing its chlamydia caseload by as much as 56 percent over five years. Conversely, widespread lack of screening is one reason why chlamydia rates in this country are 100 times higher than in Sweden and some other European countries. In one survey of American patients, less than 12 percent had ever discussed STDs with their primary care physicians. The Jacobs Institute for Women's Health, located in Washington, D.C., notes that managed care organizations are well-positioned to adopt screening policies that will affect large populations but that their potential is diminished by patients' doubts about the health plan's ability or willingness to protect confidentiality. In fact, many patients who have health insurance prefer to go to public clinics if they have concerns about STDs, for reasons of anonymity.

Partner notification is an important tool for controlling the spread of chlamydia and other STDs. One study calculated that locating and treating the infected female partners of 1,000 chlamydia-infected men would save $247,000 by preventing 64 cases of PID. Locating and treating the infected male partners of 1,000 chlamydia-infected women—thus protecting the women from reinfection—would save $33,000 in averted PID. Both NCHSTP and the Jacobs Institute have observed that insurance barriers can hinder such efforts. They suggest that Managed Care Organizations (MCOs) work out a protocol whereby they can be reimbursed by another company or the government for notifying and treating infected partners who do not belong to their plans.

Gonorrhea, which infected an estimated 800,000 individuals in 1995, raises many of the same cost issues as chlamydia, and the average expense per case is similar. Treatment consists of a single dose of antibiotic, which may cost $4.67 (cefixime) or $8.60 (ceftriaxone); but the longer a case goes undiagnosed, the more likely it is to result in PID. An increasing number of gonorrhea strains are resistant to antibiotics, resulting in more treatment failures and potentially very serious cost increases down the road. Syphilis infects an estimated 100,000 Americans each year. It has been in decline for decades, to the point where routine premarital screening is now far from being cost effective. However, one study found that syphilis screening of ER patients with other STDs was highly economical—costing only $105 per case identified. Nevertheless, neonatal syphilis, transmitted to infants by

untreated mothers, cost an estimated $12.4 million in 1990, or about 20 percent of the total economic burden of the disease.

## The Cost of Long-Term Treatment

Human papillomavirus (HPV) infection, genital herpes and hepatitis B infection are incurable, but treatment can suppress the symptoms and lower the risk of transmission. A percentage of cases resolve of themselves.

HPV causes genital warts and is the reason for an estimated half million physician visits annually. Although no global cost estimates are available, patients and physicians treat these lesions in a variety of ways, from inexpensive topical preparations to expensive interferon injections and laser surgery. The major concern with genital warts, as well as the major cost implications, result from strong evidence linking some strains of HPV to cervical cancer. One study has estimated that human papillomavirus causes 75 percent of all cases, which would translate to an annual $500 million in cancer-related costs.

Herpes simplex lesions prompt an estimated 200,000 to 500,000 physician visits per year. Standard treatment for the initial outbreak is a two-week high-dose course of the antiviral drug acyclovir, at a wholesale price of about $70. Subsequently, continuous therapy to keep the sores from recurring costs about $1,300 wholesale. Women with herpes sores during childbirth can easily transmit the infection to their newborns—with potentially serious and costly complications. This is a very common concern, since an estimated 5 percent of pregnant women have a history of herpes. A recent study compared prevention strategies, consisting of giving the mother acyclovir in the third trimester to resolve all lesions (and hopefully lower the viral potency of any that persist), and delivery by Cesarean section to lower the amount of exposure to virus in the mother's genital tract. The strategy that was most effective clinically—using the drug and C-section delivery even if there were no lesions—prevented 85 percent of neonatal infections, at a cost of $493,000 per infection averted.

Hepatitis B infection is transmitted by addicts' hypodermic needles as well as sexually; health care workers are also at risk. Treatment with alpha 2b interferon is expensive: approximately $5,000 wholesale for a 16-week course to suppress liver inflammation. The total costs for hepatitis B include interventions for cirrhosis and liver cancer: an estimated $138 million in 1984—the latest figures available—according to a 1997 Institute of Medicine report. In the future, much of the cost of the disease may be mitigated, thanks to a hepatitis B vaccine now included in the standard childhood immunizations and given to adults at high risk.

# THE PROBLEM OF STDS AMONG ADOLESCENTS AND YOUNG ADULTS

Sue Alford and Gary Linnen

Despite a decline in sexual activity among high school students, sexually transmitted disease (STD) rates among adolescents remain high, write Sue Alford and Gary Linnen. In the following selection, the authors have compiled some startling statistics on the scope of the STD epidemic among Americans under the age of twenty-one. They reveal, for example, that 52 percent of reported HIV cases occur in males between thirteen and nineteen years of age. The authors also report that although condom use has increased, many sexually active high school students still fail to use them. To stem the epidemic, the authors suggest culturally-sensitive prevention strategies that involve peers and family. Alford and Linnen compiled this report for Advocates for Youth, an organization that provides information and advocates policies that help young people make informed and responsible decisions about their reproductive and sexual health.

One-quarter of all new HIV infections in the U.S. are estimated to occur in young people under the age of 21. Each day, between 27 and 54 young people under the age of 20 in the U.S. are infected with HIV. UNAIDS [the United Nations' program for addressing the global AIDS crisis] estimates that, of the 30 million people living with HIV worldwide, at least 10 million are between the ages of 10 and 24.

Although declining sexual activity rates and increased condom use among sexually active youth sound a hopeful note, the increasing HIV/AIDS epidemic among young people of color and young men who have sex with men (YMSM) underscores the need for more focused, gender- and culturally appropriate prevention programs which build skills, enhance self-esteem, and promote behavior change.

## HIV/STD Rates for Adolescents Remain High

By December 1997, 3,130 AIDS cases among people ages 13 to 19 in the U.S. were reported to the Centers for Disease Control and Preven-

From "Adolescents, HIV/AIDS, and Other STDs," by Sue Alford and Gary Linnen, www.advocatesforyouth.org, November 1998. Copyright © 1998 by Advocates for Youth. Reprinted with permission.

tion (CDC); among people ages 20 to 24, 22,953 AIDS cases were reported. Because of the long incubation period between infection with HIV and AIDS diagnosis, most of those in the 20- to 24-year age group were infected during their teens.

The percentage of adolescent AIDS cases among female teens in the U.S. has risen from 14 percent in 1987 to 49 percent of all adolescent cases reported in 1997.

Through 1997, African American and Latina teens accounted for 82 percent of the cumulative AIDS cases among young women ages 13 to 19 in the U.S.

Among males 13 to 19, 41 percent of AIDS cases and 52 percent of HIV cases reported to the Centers for Disease Control and Prevention (CDC) in 1997 were among YMSM and YMSM injecting drug users.

HIV infection is the leading cause of death among all people in the U.S. ages 25 to 44 and the sixth leading cause among all people ages 15 to 24. Among those ages 15 to 24, HIV infection is the seventh leading cause of death among white males and females, sixth among Latino males and females, fifth among African American males, and third among African American females.

Between 1993 and 1996, gonorrhea rates decreased 36 percent among males and 11 percent among females ages 15 to 19. Nevertheless, among women, those ages 15 to 19 had the highest gonorrhea rate; among men, those ages 15 to 19 had the second highest gonorrhea rate.

In one study of urban adolescent women, 15.6 percent were infected with human papilloma virus (HPV), 11 percent were infected with chlamydia, seven percent with gonorrhea, and over five percent with trichomoniasis. The study confirmed that cervical HPV is acquired predominately by sexual contact, often soon after the onset of sexual activity.

## Risk Behaviors Decline Unequally

The percentage of U.S. high school students who have had sexual intercourse has decreased from 54.1 percent in 1991 to 48.4 percent in 1997. However, rates did not decline significantly among female students or among Latinos.

Sexually active high school students' use of condoms at most recent sexual intercourse rose from 46.2 percent in 1991 to 56.8 percent in 1997. However, even the improved condom use statistics demonstrate that 41.1 percent of African American, 60 percent of Latina, and 50.8 percent of white sexually active female students failed to use condoms at last sexual intercourse.

Research indicates that older male partners present a greater HIV transmission risk than adolescent males because they are more likely to have had multiple sex partners, to have had varied sexual and drug use experiences, and to be infected with HIV. While older men's engaging in sexual relations with younger women is widespread, a disproportionately high percentage of adult men with minor partners in a nationally representative survey were African American and Latino.

Risk of HIV infection is higher among urban African American and Latina women who are living in or near poverty because of high rates of injection drug use in these communities. A small proportion of U.S. high school students put themselves and their sexual partners at risk of HIV infection through injection drug use. Nationwide, 2.1 percent of students in 1997 had injected drugs.

In one study of sexually active female adolescents, 81 percent responded that they had "never done anything that could give them a chance of getting AIDS." Most estimated their chances of infection to be "very low" (36 percent) or "nonexistent" (37 percent). Main reasons for assessing personal risk these ways included current monogamy, belief in a sexual partner's safety and fidelity, belief in the ability to choose partners carefully, use of condoms, and nonuse of injection drugs.

In the U.S., knowledge regarding STDs is low even though teens exhibit greater knowledge than adults. In one poll, only 12 percent of American teens and four percent of adults were aware that STDs infect as many as one-fifth of people in the U.S. Twenty six percent of adults and 42 percent of teens could not name an STD other than HIV/AIDS.

In a San Francisco study of young men who have sex with men (YMSM), 28.7 percent of those ages 17 to 19 and 34.3 percent of those ages 20 to 22 reported unprotected anal intercourse during the last six months. A similar Los Angeles study found 55.3 percent of YMSM reporting unprotected anal intercourse in the last six months.

In a 1996 study of 1,781 YMSM, 38 percent reported having unprotected anal sex, and 27 percent reported having unprotected receptive anal sex.

## The Influence of Cultural and Community Norms

Cultural and community norms are very important in HIV prevention interventions. In a survey of community-based organizations working with adolescents on condom negotiation, the single most frequently discussed problem was gender norms which prevent females from asking about their partners' sexual history and insisting on condom use, usually because of real or perceived lack of power in relation to males.

In the same study of community-based organizations, researchers noted that young people sometimes value risk behavior as a "badge of maturity."

Because of a high degree of homophobia among teens and because some young people experiment, researchers and service providers agree that it is necessary when discussing risks for HIV or STD with youth to ask about same-sex sexual behaviors rather than about sexual orientation.

Consistent condom use among Latinos is hampered by the opposition to birth control of the Catholic Church (the religion of 75 percent of Latinos) and by cultural attitudes about gender roles and condoms.

## The Prevention Strategies

In a review of 35 programs around the world, the World Health Organization found that programs that teach only abstinence were less effective than programs that promote the delay of first sexual intercourse and teach about safer sex practices, such as contraception and condom use, at delaying sexual intercourse among youth who have not yet had sex and at improving contraceptive use among sexually active teens.

Peer-assisted interventions enhance HIV knowledge and decrease risk behaviors. One analysis found that peer-based interventions can reduce HIV risk-associated behavior, increase condom acquisition and condom use, and decrease unprotected sexual intercourse, frequency of sexual intercourse, and the number of sexual partners.

A national survey in 1997 found that family factors are significantly associated with delaying sexual intercourse. Among young people who have not yet initiated sex, these family factors include high levels of connection—teens' perception of receiving warmth, love, and caring from their parents—and parental disapproval of teen sexual activity. Among sexually active youth, the study found that a greater number of shared activities with parents is protective.

A 1998 study demonstrates that interactive risk reduction counseling is effective in substantially reducing unprotected sexual intercourse by increasing condom use and in reducing the incidence of STDs among STD clinic clients.

# STDs Can Harm Babies

Lorie A. Parch

Countless pregnant women are unaware they are living with a sexually transmitted disease (STD) and are ignorant of the harm these diseases can cause their babies, writes Lorie A. Parch in the following selection. Many women often assume that they will be screened for STDs as part of their prenatal care, Parch explains, when in reality, health care providers only test those women perceived to be at risk. Unfortunately, even women in monogamous marriages are susceptible because their partners may have contracted an STD—which can remain dormant for years—before they were married. Parch outlines several STDs, their symptoms, the risks to mothers and their babies, and treatment options. To avoid birth complications, Parch asserts, women must be aware of STDs and the potential impact these diseases can have on their babies. Parch is a freelance writer from New York and a *Baby Talk* contributing editor.

After sailing through her third pregnancy, Lis, a 37-year-old mother from upstate New York, gave birth to a boy in January. As she held her new son, Simon, he seemed happy and healthy, weighing in at 9 pounds, 1 ounce, and racking up a 9 out of a possible 10 points on the Apgar scale of newborn health. Five days later, his first infant checkup was equally reassuring—until the pediatrician noticed small bumps on his face, near his eyes. He inspected them carefully, then turned to Lis and her husband and asked if either of them had herpes.

Lis's body went cold. Two years earlier, her husband had developed small sores and had unexpectedly been diagnosed with genital herpes. "The doctor told us that my husband could have gotten the virus years before and never had an outbreak," she recalls. "But no one ever suggested that I get tested. No one ever said to me 'You could have herpes and not know it.'" Unfortunately, like up to 90 percent of people with herpes, Lis didn't know she was infected because she had never had any symptoms. Simon was rushed to a nearby medical center where a DNA spinal tap test confirmed that he had neonatal herpes, a condition which usually results in severe central nervous system damage and often in death. He spent the next three weeks in the hospital, where he underwent another spinal tap and received intravenous doses of acyclovir, an antiviral drug.

Fortunately, Simon beat extraordinary odds and was able to go home. "By some miracle we caught this early and he was treated soon enough that he never got sick," says Lis. Now, at 7 months old, Simon is thriving, doing everything babies his age are meant to do. But his parents wish they could spare others the terrifying experience they had. "We spent the first four weeks of our seemingly healthy baby's life in an intensive care unit because of the devastating effects this virus has on a newborn."

## A Silent Epidemic

Sexually transmitted diseases (STDs) are perhaps the most overlooked threat to babies today. According to the Centers for Disease Control and Prevention (CDC), 65 million Americans are now living with an incurable STD and 15 million more are infected each year. It's estimated that one in four pregnant women has herpes and that three out of four women will contract human papillomavirus (HPV), the virus with strains that can cause genital warts and cervical cancer. Countless others live with curable STDs like chlamydia or gonorrhea but don't know it—and don't understand the harm they can pose to a newborn.

Because these diseases often do not cause noticeable symptoms, many pregnant women don't find out they have an STD until it's too late. Untreated, these infections can cause preterm labor and the related complications of low birth weight, in addition to blindness, pneumonia, brain damage, developmental disabilities, and even death. STDs can be hazardous for the mother as well: Many can compromise a woman's fertility or increase the risk of the transmission of HIV, the virus that causes AIDS.

Most people aren't aware of these dangers or of the severity of the STD epidemic. It is a silent—and potentially deadly—threat. "Pregnant women are more likely to know about the remote risk of contracting toxoplasmosis, [a congenital disease that can cause blindness and brain lumage], from changing the kitty litter during pregnancy than about the dangerous ways an STD can affect their pregnancy and their baby," says Linda Alexander, Ph.D., president of the American Social Health Association (ASHA), the country's leading clearinghouse for STD information.

Because they are so widespread and often without symptoms, STDs don't discriminate—even women like Lis, who is in a monogamous marriage, are vulnerable. "The single most important message about STDs is that everyone is at risk—it doesn't matter what your current or past sexual behavior is," warns Lyn Finelli, Ph.D., a former epidemiologist in the division of STD prevention at the CDC in Atlanta who is now the chief of surveillance in the viral hepatitis division.

Many pregnant women incorrectly assume that they'll be screened for STDs as part of their prenatal care, but the truth is that routine tests are offered only for hepatitis B, syphilis, and HIV. Beyond these three tests, the American College of Obstetricians and Gynecologists and the CDC advise testing expectant mothers for other STDs (such as chlamydia, gonorrhea, herpes, and HPV) only if a health care provider believes a woman is at increased risk. That means a woman has told her doctor that she has more than one sexual partner, a partner who has multiple partners, a history of STD infection or IV drug use, or that she was the victim of a sexual assault.

These screening practices don't go far enough, argues Alexander, who believes that pregnant women should be tested for all STDs or at least educated about them during a prenatal visit. "Women should understand their risk from all infections," she says. "Unfortunately, the stigma of STDs keeps us from dealing with them."

Perhaps the greatest tragedy of all is that most STDs can be easily detected and managed—if not completely cured—during pregnancy. If an STD is diagnosed before delivery, the health of both mother and child can almost always be protected: Bacterial diseases such as chlamydia, gonorrhea, and trichomoniasis can be wiped out with antibiotics, while viral STDs like herpes and HPV can be effectively controlled, reducing the likelihood that an infant will contract the condition. And further advances in the prevention, diagnosis, and treatment of STDs are on the horizon. A vaccine to prevent herpes and another to prevent certain strains of HPV are currently in development. Foams or jellies known as microbicides, which would protect a woman against STDs but still allow her to become pregnant, are being tested as well.

Following are the facts you'll need to understand the effects of STDs and to recognize any noticeable symptoms. . . . "Women will have to be proactive," says James McGregor, M.D., C.M., professor of obstetrics and gynecology at the University of Colorado in Denver. "Talking about STDs is like preparing a birth plan: In order to have it implemented, you have to come in prepared."

## Chlamydia

Stats: An estimated 3 million new cases of chlamydia are diagnosed each year, making it the most common bacterial infection in the United States. Rates are higher in women younger than 25 years old.

Symptoms: Though 75 percent of women with chlamydia do not have any symptoms, there may be painful or frequent urination or vaginal discharge, usually occurring within two days to three weeks of exposure. This may be accompanied by pelvic or abdominal pain during sex, fever or chills, nausea, vomiting, burning or itching in the vaginal area, joint pain, or a sore throat.

Testing: Identification of chlamydia can be done through a DNA test (which looks for the DNA of the chlamydia organism), a culture test of cervical cells, or a urine sample.

Risk to Mothers: As many as 40 percent of women with untreated chlamydia will develop pelvic inflammatory disease (PID)—an infection of the uterus, fallopian tubes, and ovaries—with 1 in 5 women with PID becoming infertile. Chlamydia also increases the risk of an ectopic pregnancy, which occurs when the embryo implants in the fallopian tube instead of in the uterus.

Risk to Babies: If the bacteria is passed to a baby during delivery, it can cause pneumonia or eye infections such as conjunctivitis. Chlamydia can also cause premature rupture of the membranes, preterm birth, and miscarriage.

Treatment: Antibiotics.

## Gonorrhea

Stats: The CDC estimates that there are 650,000 cases each year.

Symptoms: Signs of gonorrhea are the same as those for chlamydia, though half of infections in women do not cause any symptoms.

Testing: In women, a culture of the cervix is usually taken. Testing for chlamydia and gonorrhea at the same time is common since the two infections often appear together.

Risk to Mothers: If not treated, gonorrhea can lead to PID in 10 to 20 percent of affected women. It can also cause joint pain, arthritis, and affect the heart and brain.

Risk to Babies: Gonorrhea can cause miscarriage and, if it infects a newborn's eyes, can lead to blindness.

Treatment: Antibiotics. Many states recommend precautionary treatment of all newborns' eyes with silver nitrate drops at birth to prevent infection.

## Herpes

Stats: There are 1 million new herpes infections each year, with an estimated 45 million Americans already infected. About 1,500 newborns are infected annually with neonatal herpes, according to Zane Brown, M.D., a professor of obstetrics and gynecology at the University of Washington in Seattle and a leading authority on neonatal herpes.

Symptoms: While as many as 90 percent of people with herpes do not have symptoms, those infected can experience sores (internal or external) that last two to three weeks, itching or burning, vaginal discharge, a feeling of pressure in the abdomen, fever, headache, or pain in the legs, buttocks, or genitals.

Testing: If you have symptoms, a culture can be taken to confirm or rule out herpes, and blood tests can determine which strain you have—Herpes Simplex Virus 1 (HSV-1), which usually causes oral herpes (in the form of cold sores), or Herpes Simplex Virus 2 (HSV-2), which typically causes genital herpes. Without any symptoms, blood tests are available to determine if you have herpes, though false positives can sometimes occur.

Risk to Mothers: A pregnant woman with long-standing herpes may find that outbreaks are more frequent and severe while she's expecting. Medication to suppress outbreaks is usually administered late in pregnancy, but if a woman has herpes sores at the time of delivery, a cesarean section will likely need to be done.

Risk to Babies: If a woman acquires herpes before becoming pregnant or early in her pregnancy, the chances of the infection harming her unborn child are small. That's because she has time to build up immunity to the virus and can pass that immunity to her baby. If an expectant mother is first infected with herpes in her last trimester, her baby has a 30 to 50 percent chance of contracting neonatal herpes, which can be life-threatening to an infant because the mother has had less time to build up immunity to the virus and pass protective antibodies to her baby. Fortunately, what often appears to be an initial infection during pregnancy is in fact a recurrence and less risky for a baby. Though neonatal herpes is rare, it can cause eye and throat infections in addition to inflammation of the brain, central nervous system damage, developmental delays, and death. Signs of infection (which usually occur two to three weeks later) include sores around the eyes, irritability, lethargy, poor feeding, and seizures.

Treatment: There's no getting rid of the herpes virus, but outbreaks can be controlled with antiviral medications such as acyclovir. A 15-year pregnancy registry for acyclovir found no elevated risk of birth defects in babies.

## Human Immunodeficiency Virus (HIV)

Stats: According to the March of Dimes, 1 in 625 pregnant women are HIV-positive and an estimated 6,000 babies are born to HIV-infected mothers each year. In 1998 (the most recent year for which figures are available), fewer than 300 of these babies became infected with the AIDS virus.

Symptoms: Those infected with HIV usually do not have symptoms because it takes time for the virus to wear down the immune system. In some cases a woman will have a brief, flu-like illness. Untreated over time, HIV depletes immunity, increasing vulnerability to infection and disease.

Testing: A health care provider can draw blood or take a sample of saliva to test for HIV, or, if you prefer private testing, the FDA-approved Home Access Test is available in pharmacies, online at www.homeaccess.com, or by calling 847/781-2500.

Risk to Mothers: Most women diagnosed with HIV who receive treatment feel fine during pregnancy. If an HIV-positive expectant mother does not receive medication or begins treatment late in pregnancy, she'll be more likely to have a c-section to reduce her child's exposure to the virus. Because HIV can be passed through breast milk, new mothers with HIV or AIDS shouldn't nurse.

Risk to Babies: Babies can acquire HIV from their mothers during labor and delivery, or in utero. With the advent of the drug zidovudine (AZT, ZDV, Retrovir), the mother-to-baby transmission rate has been greatly reduced, from approximately 25 percent of babies born to HIV-infected mothers before 1994 to less than 5 percent. About 20 percent of infected infants develop AIDS in the first year of life and die before the age of 4. The remainder usually develop AIDS before age 6. These infants and children are at risk for poor growth, serious bacterial infections, pneumonia, neurologic problems, and developmental delays.

Treatment: Zidovudine helps prevent transmission of the virus from mother to baby. Antiretroviral drugs can also strengthen a woman's immunity and further reduce the risk of transmission. A pregnancy registry is being maintained that will monitor the effects of these drugs on both women and newborns.

## Human Papillomavirus (HPV)

Stats: HPV is the most common STD in the U.S., with an estimated 75 percent of the reproductive-age population infected. Twenty million Americans have HPV, with 5.5 million new cases diagnosed each year.

Symptoms: In some people, HPV can cause genital warts.

Testing: A Pap smear, which can detect changes in cervical cells, can indicate an HPV infection or the early stages of cervical cancer, particularly if the changes are dramatic. For minor Pap changes, a follow-up DNA test can confirm or rule out the presence of HPV. But testing for HPV in pregnancy if genital warts are not present is usually unnecessary because the virus is so prevalent and the risk of transmission is so low, says Thomas Cox, M.D., executive medical director of the HPV and Cervical Cancer Prevention Resource Center at ASHA and director of the gynecology clinic at the University of California in Santa Barbara. If you have warts that have not been diagnosed, however, you should see a doctor and be tested.

Risk to Mothers: A woman previously infected with HPV may get genital warts for the first time during pregnancy or find that her current warts grow significantly. Of the approximately 70 strains of HPV, the ones that cause warts (strains 6 and 11) are the least worrisome. Strains 16, 18, 31, and 45 account for 80 percent of all cervical cancers.

Risk to Babies: The risk of HPV transmission during delivery is very low; less than 1 percent of affected women pass it to their babies. In these infants, there is a slight chance that they will later develop the virus in their larynx (voice box). If a woman has very large genital warts close to her due date, a c-section may be considered.

Treatment: Several treatments for genital warts that are often given to women who are not pregnant haven't been proven safe for use in pregnancy, says Dr. Cox. It's possible that your OB might freeze or laser the warts or put acid on them since these procedures are safe during pregnancy. Many healthy women appear to get rid of HPV over time or at least to suppress it to the point where it is no longer a threat to them, their partner, or their children.

## Syphilis

Stats: Approximately 70,000 Americans get syphilis each year, though infection rates are significantly higher in some southern states and in African-Americans. In 1999 there were 556 reported cases of congenital syphilis in infants who acquired the disease from their mothers during pregnancy or delivery.

Symptoms: The primary stage of syphilis is characterized by a small, firm, round, painless sore (called a chancre) that appears from 10 to 90 days after infection at the place where the bacterium entered the body; the sore lasts one to five weeks. If not treated, the appearance of a non-itching rash on one or more parts of the body indicates the start of the second stage of syphilis. There may be rough, "copper penny" spots on the palms of the hands and bottoms of the feet. Most pregnant women with syphilis are asymptomatic, says Dr. McGregor.

Testing: In many states, a syphilis screen—a blood test—is the only routine prenatal STD test.

Risk to Mothers: Third-stage syphilis (called latency) begins to attack the internal organs, eventually leading to blindness, dementia, and lack of muscle coordination, among other complications.

Risk to Babies: A pregnant woman with untreated syphilis has a 40 percent chance of a stillbirth or having a baby who dies shortly after delivery. If a mother-to-be doesn't receive treatment, or receives it too late in pregnancy, there's a 40 to 70 percent chance she'll deliver a syphilitic baby. Signs of an infection include sores, runny nose (sometimes bloody), jaundice, a small head, anemia, a swollen liver, slimy patches in the mouth, and inflammation of the bones in the arms and legs. A newborn may not show signs of infection until 3 to 8 weeks after birth.

Treatment: Penicillin.

## Trichomoniasis

Stats: The parasite which causes trichomoniasis affects an estimated 5 million women each year.

Symptoms: The condition, often called "trich," can cause a foul-smelling or green vaginal discharge, vaginal itching, or redness within six months of infection. Other symptoms can include painful sexual intercourse, lower abdominal discomfort, and the urge to urinate.

Testing: A health care provider can diagnose trichomoniasis by examining vaginal discharge.

Risk to Mothers: Trichomoniasis can cause preterm labor.

Risk to Babies: Preterm labor can cause a baby to have a low birth weight. According to the CDC, mother-to-baby transmission of the parasite is rare, but symptoms in an infected infant include fever, as well as a vaginal discharge in girls.

Treatment: Antibiotics after the first trimester. (The medicine is not safe for use during the early months of pregnancy.)

The STD epidemic is an undeniable health threat to infants today. Unlike other epidemics, however, it is one that can be easily controlled. If pregnant women insist on being tested for these diseases, in most cases STDs can become what they should be—a nuisance, not a danger. Armed with the right information and a doctor's guidance, a woman with an STD can help keep herself—and her baby—healthy.

# Women Who Have Sex with Women Are at Risk for STDs

Greta R. Bauer and Seth L. Welles

Many believe that women who have sex with women (WSW) are at low risk of contracting sexually transmitted diseases (STDs), yet little research has been conducted to effectively assess the actual risk for these women, write Greta R. Bauer and Seth L. Welles. According to the authors, however, the results of a study designed to assess the STD risk of WSW reveal that they are in fact at risk of contracting STDs. In the following selection, the authors discuss the study's methods, results, and conclusions. WSW, the authors assert, do report a significant prevalence of STDs. Unfortunately, they state, WSW are unlikely to obtain STD testing and, therefore, many with STDs do not receive necessary treatment. These results, they argue, suggest that WSW be provided with information to make informed decisions about their health. Bauer is with the Division of Epidemiology at the University of Minnesota School of Public Health in Minneapolis. Welles is professor of epidemiology at Boston University School of Public Health.

Although the AIDS epidemic has catalyzed research on disease transmission through anal and vaginal intercourse, few studies have addressed transmission between women. Even fewer studies have examined female-to-female risk of sexually transmitted diseases (STDs) that may be transmitted more readily than HIV. While a 1981 study produced no evidence of current infection with gonorrhea, chlamydia, syphilis, or cervical herpes among 148 lesbians, subsequent reports have identified several STDs as transmissible through same-sex female contact, including herpes, trichomoniasis, human papillomavirus, and HIV. These reports have identified only transmissibility; additional research is required to elucidate the magnitude of risk of STD transmission through female-female sexual contact.

## The Difficulties of Assessing Risk

An estimated 6.7% of American women have engaged in same-sex sexual behavior after the age of 15 years, and 3.6% have engaged in

Excerpted from "Beyond Assumptions of Negligible Risk: Sexually Transmitted Diseases and Women Who Have Sex with Women," by Greta R. Bauer and Seth L. Welles, *American Journal of Public Health*, August 2001. Copyright © 2001 by *American Journal of Public Health*. Reprinted with permission.

such behavior within the preceding 5 years. While recent research emphasizes the need to consider risk from male partners regardless of sexual orientation identity, disagreement exists among clinicians and public health workers over assessment of disease transmission risk resulting from female-female contact and which behavioral precautions and testing measures should be considered. Insufficient research has been done to estimate the risks for non-HIV STDs. Nevertheless, a perception exists that women who have sex with women (WSW), or even lesbians as an identity group, are at low or no risk for STDs. Among 1,925 women participating in the National Lesbian Health Care Survey, less than a quarter reported that they worried about contracting STDs.

In addition to this perception that they are at low risk, other factors may result in a lower likelihood that lesbians and other WSW will obtain STD testing. As a result of negative experiences and expectations, lesbians are less likely to use health care resources, particularly preventive health care. This is relevant not only to acknowledging the unmet health care needs of this population but also to interpreting research that frequently relies on self-report data containing undiagnosed asymptomatic cases, resulting in underestimates of disease.

The difficulties in defining and studying "hidden" populations such as WSW have been well documented. Studies have involved samples from clinics, women's music festivals, a lesbian softball league, multiple public venues, and magazine readerships. While all such studies contribute valuable information in an understudied area, inferences apply only to specific source populations.

## Gathering the Data

The current study built on a small but growing body of research by estimating associations between female-female sexual behaviors and STDs after control for female-male sexual behavior and other variables independently associated with STDs. Unlike most previous studies in this area, this study examined individual-level data gathered in a community setting with a method designed to reduce bias. We also estimated associations with regular STD testing to provide information that may be useful in prevention efforts and in understanding how bias might affect results in studies of WSW.

We sought to estimate the predictive value of sexual exposure from female partners in a sample of women self-identifying as lesbian, bisexual, and heterosexual, the majority of whom reported a history of both male and female sexual partners. The magnitude of the association between female-female risk factors and outcome variables can be estimated when known risk factors and confounding variables, including male-female risk factors, are controlled.

When one is considering risks from sexual exposure, several factors are relevant. Number of partners represents the probability of contact with an infected partner. A measure of exposure provides additional information, in that increasing numbers of sexual exposures with infected partners increase the probability of disease transmission. Specific sexual practices are also relevant; for example, using latex barriers or engaging in lower risk sexual behaviors reduces the probability of transmission from an infected partner.

All subjects were recruited from the Twin Cities Gay/Lesbian/Bisexual/Transgender Pride Festival, held in June 1997. With an estimated attendance of 100,000, the festival represented a diverse cross section of the Minneapolis–St. Paul community [also known as the Twin Cities]. The 2-day free event offered easy access, child-friendly events, extensive disability accessibility, and a minimal focus on alcohol; these conditions provided a population with a diversity of risk for STDs. . . .

Subjects reported lifetime totals in terms of both male and female sexual partners; transgender sexual partners were classified by anatomic sex rather than gender identity. Subjects estimated their average monthly sexual frequency with female partners as well as total lifetime months spent in sexual relationships with women; these values were multiplied to derive an estimate of lifetime sexual exposure through female contact. An identical process was used in assessing male sexual partners.

A dichotomous variable was derived to indicate higher risk sexual contact with men, defined as unprotected vaginal or anal intercourse in "about half" or more of the subject's sexual exposures with male partners. No comparable variable was calculated for female partners, because inadequate information is available as to what constellation of behaviors might constitute "higher risk."

A continuous variable was derived for lifetime months of binge drinking. This behavior was defined as regularly (at least once per week) consuming 5 or more drinks on the same day.

Subjects indicated whether they had ever been diagnosed with the following STDs: HIV, hepatitis B virus, gonorrhea, syphilis, chlamydia, genital warts, genital herpes, and trichomoniasis. Pelvic inflammatory disease was also included, because it generally results from untreated chlamydia or gonorrhea. A dichotomous summary variable was created to indicate lifetime diagnosis of any STD. Subjects also indicated frequency of STD testing with regular testing defined as at least once per year. . . .

## Examining the Results

The age range was 18 to 83 years, with a median age of 31 years. The ethnic identity of the sample reflected population demographics in the Twin Cities metropolitan area. Women in the sample were well educated, and 69% self-identified as lesbian. A history of both male and female sexual partners was reported by 69%.

That a majority of the sample self-identified as lesbian and a majority also indicated a history of both male and female sexual partners indicates that sexual orientation identity and sexual partner history were not neatly congruent. Among lesbians, 74% reported a history of both male and female sexual partners, while 24% reported only female partners. Ninety percent of bisexual women reported a history of both male and female sexual partners, and 8% reported only male partners.

While all women who reported only female partners self-identified as lesbian, the relationship between sexual orientation identity and sexual partner history was not as clear for women with other partner histories. Women in this sample who reported only male sexual partners appeared in all orientation groups, as did women who reported both male and female sexual partners and women who reported no sexual partners.

Frequencies of specific STDs were calculated. Twenty-one percent of subjects reported ever having been diagnosed with an STD. No subjects reported HIV or syphilis, both low-prevalence diseases in this geographic area. Frequencies for other STDs were as follows: hepatitis B, 1%; gonorrhea, 2%; chlamydia, 6%; genital warts, 8%; genital herpes, 5%; trichomoniasis, 6%; and pelvic inflammatory disease, 5%. Eighteen percent of the women reported regular STD testing.

Of the subgroup of women who reported only female sexual partners, 13% reported a history of STDs. STDs reported by this group included chlamydia, genital warts, trichomoniasis, and pelvic inflammatory disease. Among women self-identifying as lesbians, 15% reported ever having been diagnosed with an STD. . . .

Women who report sexual relations only with other women do become infected with STDs. The group in this study reported a 13% lifetime prevalence of STDs, a rate clearly not representative of "no risk." In addition, only 4 of these 39 women reported regular testing for STDs; thus, this group may have included a disproportionately large number of cases of undiagnosed STDs.

In the overall sample, frequency of female-female sexual exposure was independently associated with increased odds of STDs when female-male sexual behavior was controlled for. This represents the first estimation of magnitude of risk due specifically to sexual behavior between women.

Of the 5 sexual behavior variables tested as predictors of a history of STD diagnosis, only lifetime number of sexual exposures with female partners and lifetime number of male sexual partners were independently predictive in the final model. Although positively predictive in the bivariate analysis, high-risk sexual behavior with male partners dropped out of the final model. Age was also a positive predictor in the bivariate analysis, as would be expected with a cumulative outcome variable. However, it was not significant when included in the final model, indicating that the model variables better explained the outcome.

It is of interest that number of sexual exposures was predictive for female partners and number of partners was predictive for male partners. One possible explanation is that the per-contact probability of transmission is lower overall for female-female transmission, and thus more exposures are required, on average, to transmit disease. This explanation is biologically plausible in the case of diseases, such as chlamydia, that infect the cervix: although transmission from penile tip to cervix can easily occur through penile-vaginal intercourse, transmission from cervix to cervix would be less direct. The explanation is less biologically plausible in the case of diseases that may require only external contact for transmission (e.g., human papillomavirus, herpes simplex virus). Future studies examining individual STDs or STDs grouped by site of infection could clarify this issue.

## The Likelihood of STD Testing

In the model predicting regular STD testing, increases in male partners and in male sexual exposures predicted an increased likelihood of regular testing. Female sexual partners and sexual exposures did not influence likelihood of testing and were not included in the model. Conversely, older age predicted a decreased likelihood of testing. This may have been due to an accurate assessment of risk, in that older individuals may more likely be monogamous, or it may have been due to a lower awareness of risk among older individuals than among the younger ones who came of age after the emergence of the AIDS epidemic.

Women self-identifying as lesbian were only 27% as likely to obtain regular STD testing as women self-identifying as bisexual or heterosexual. When age, number of male partners, and number of male sexual exposures were controlled for, lesbian identity was suggestive of decreased testing, with lesbians 47% as likely to obtain testing. This suggests that women self-identifying as lesbians may still be less likely to obtain testing, even after their lower risk sexual histories with male partners have been taken into account. Future studies should examine this issue in greater detail. A low frequency of preventive health care use by lesbians agrees with existing research. Moreover, it is consistent with perceptions within lesbian communities and within the health care professions that STD testing is not critical because sexual relations between women involve negligible risk.

Although the present methodology was designed to produce a sample as representative as possible of the study geographic area, sources of bias must be considered. For example, this was a convenience sample, and only individuals who attended the 1997 Twin Cities Gay/Lesbian/Bisexual/Transgender Pride Festival were selected to participate. Depending on prevalence rates of underlying risk factors, STD prevalence rates can be expected to vary between this and other populations. Institutionalized individuals were not included, nor were extremely "closeted" individuals who are inaccessible to any research on this population. Furthermore, probability of selection increased with length of time spent at the festival. Nevertheless, sampling was done with consideration of the factors that make this event uniquely conducive to the goal of representativeness and that minimize selection bias.

Lesbians in this sample were not synonymous with WSW. Rather, WSW identified across all sexual orientation identities. This is consistent with the existing literature. Understanding the complex relationship between identity and behavior is crucial in interpreting data in this study and other studies of WSW.

Combined, the analyses conducted in this study indicate that the risk faced by WSW regarding STDs and their consequences is characterized not only by a significant risk for contracting STDs from both female and male partners but also by a corresponding lack of testing. This finding has important clinical and public health implications. Physicians and other clinicians should consider risk of transmission between women in health care decision making; decisions to administer STD testing and Papanicolaou tests should be made considering this risk and should not be based solely on current or past involvement with male sexual partners.

From a public health perspective, the perception that sexual relations between women are low risk or even risk free needs to be addressed. WSW, including lesbians as an identity group, should be provided with accurate information so that they can make informed decisions regarding their health. To provide more complete information for such decision making, additional research needs to address precise behavioral risk factors for disease-specific sexual transmission between women.

# THE LEGAL IMPLICATIONS OF STDS

Kim Pittaway

In the following selection, Kim Pittaway argues that while failing to disclose to your partner that you have a sexually transmitted disease (STD) is certainly reprehensible, consenting adults have the responsibility to ask their partners if they are infected. Pittaway reports that although people with AIDS can now be held legally liable in Canada for not disclosing their condition to sexual partners, such laws likely would not apply to other STDs. Even though Pittaway criticizes the inherent illogic of such laws, she asserts that the law is not the only way to protect against contracting STDs. Far preferable would be to ask potential sexual partners about their health status before having sex, she argues. Pittaway is managing editor for *Chatelaine*.

It was the kind of newspaper story that's easy to miss: a 16 line item about a Manitoba man suing a former girlfriend for allegedly passing along human papilloma virus (HPV), a sexually transmitted disease (STD). He tried to have her charged with criminal assault, claiming she'd concealed her condition. When provincial prosecutors refused to lay charges, the story said he launched a civil suit. I might have skipped the news report myself but it stopped me because I'd recently heard two separate stories from women who believed they'd been infected with the herpes virus by men who hid their condition. They weren't suing; they were simply dealing with the fury of betrayal.

So, when I saw the news item, my first reaction was "Right on." I'd feel like suing too. Maybe after I keyed his car. Or trashed his record collection. Or outed his status in a screaming match at his office.

OK, like most grown-ups, I probably wouldn't do any of those last three. And I'm not sure legal action is the way to go either, though with STD rates where they are—studies suggest up to one in three Canadian women is infected with HPV and an estimated one in five Canadians has incurable herpes—it's surprising more people aren't ending up in court.

Until the past decade or so, case law came down firmly on the side of "lover beware." If you consented to sex, you consented to all the risks—

including the risk of contracting an STD—that go with having sex. But the tide started to turn for cases involving HIV, at least, in the early 1990s. In 1993, Charles Ssenyonga was tried for knowingly infecting women with HIV. Ssenyonga had deliberately infected his partners, even agreeing to wear a condom with at least one partner who asked him to, and then ripping it off just before penetration. He cheated his partners of their right to decide and he also cheated them of justice. He died before the case concluded, so a decision was never handed down.

In 1998, a new case involving HIV and consent made its way to the Supreme Court. In what became known as the *Cuerrier* decision, the court ruled that failure to disclose that you have HIV negates sexual consent. Your partner cannot consent to sex if he or she doesn't know the facts of your condition and, therefore, you commit fraud and battery by withholding this information, even if you do not pass on the virus. The court also laid out guidelines under which its decision could be applied to other STDs—basically, if the STD posed a risk of serious harm—but legal experts say in practical terms, it's unlikely to be applied to any treatable non-life-threatening STD.

"The problem is that this ruling made people with HIV targets for civil suits," says Ruth Carey, executive director of the HIV & AIDS Legal Clinic (Ontario) in Toronto. "You're in a relationship, you break up and the other person claims you never told them you were infected. It's your word against theirs." Societal biases persist around STDs and HIV in particular: only those engaged in deviant behaviour catch these diseases; no intelligent person would consent to sex with someone who had HIV. As a result, the legal cards are stacked against those with HIV, says Carey.

So what? you might say. If you've got an STD, it's up to you to make sure you don't pass it along. The problem is that under *Cuerrier*, you don't have to share HIV to be found liable—just failing to share the knowledge of your status is enough to land you in court. So, with one disease, we hold you criminally liable whether you spread the disease or not and with all others—chlamydia, gonorrhea, herpes, HPV, syphilis— we don't hold you criminally liable even if you do infect others.

There's another issue here too: an alarming number of people embarking on new relationships don't take even the most basic steps to protect against STDs. Many don't ask new partners fundamental questions: have you ever had an STD? When was the last time you were checked? Many don't insist on condoms—and although a condom isn't perfect protection, it's better than nothing. Then we feel betrayed when someone passes us something we were too embarrassed to discuss with that person in the first place.

Except in the most extreme cases—and Ssenyonga certainly fit that definition—I'm not sure the courts belong in the bedrooms of consenting adults. But common sense surely does. We can't expect the law to reclaim what we failed to protect in the first place.

CHAPTER 3

# PREVENTING AND TREATING SEXUALLY TRANSMITTED DISEASES

Contemporary Issues
Companion

# THE DEBATE OVER STD PREVENTION STRATEGIES

Gracie S. Hsu

The risk of contracting a sexually transmitted disease (STD) increases with the number of sexual partners a person has, and Americans, especially teenagers, are more promiscuous than in the past, reports Gracie S. Hsu in the following selection. For example, the percentage of teenage girls who are sexually experienced increased from 14 to 31 percent between 1971 and 1988. Although most agree that promiscuity has contributed to an epidemic rise in STDs, says Hsu, conservatives and liberals disagree on the solution to the problem. Conservatives, Hsu writes, believe promiscuity reflects society's moral decline, and only abstinence education will reinforce traditional values and reduce the transmission of STDs. Liberals, on the other hand, believe that education stressing only abstinence is unrealistic because many young people will have sex, despite dire warnings. Liberals believe that teaching youth about safe sex, including the use of condoms, is the best way to reduce the incidence of STDs. Hsu is a policy analyst specializing in adolescent sexuality and life issues at the Family Research Council in Washington, D.C.

A "hidden epidemic" is stalking America, according to the Institute of Medicine, a branch of the National Academy of Sciences.

More than 25 infectious diseases transmitted by unprecedented rates of promiscuous extramarital sexual activity are infecting at least 12 million Americans annually.

At current rates of infection, at least one in four Americans will contract a sexually transmitted disease (STD) at some point in life.

The United States bears the dubious distinction of leading the industrialized world in overall rates of STDs.

Two-thirds of the 12 million new cases a year are among men and women under age 25. Indeed, about 3 million teenagers—one in four sexually experienced adolescents—acquire an STD each year.

STDs should concern Americans because they can cause such serious consequences as cervical cancer, infertility, infection of offspring,

and death. Most people are unaware that
- an estimated 100,000 to 150,000 women become infertile each year as a result of an STD;
- half of the 88,000 ectopic pregnancies that occur each year are due to a preexisting STD infection;
- 4,500 American women die each year from cervical cancer, which is almost always caused by an STD called the human papilloma virus (HPV).

## A Stealthy Disease

"I don't think people understand how common some of these serious consequences are, particularly infertility," says Patricia Donovan, senior associate at the Alan Guttmacher Institute (AGI), a nonprofit research corporation specializing in reproductive health.

"Seventy-five percent of women with chlamydia don't have any symptoms. They don't know until 5 years later, when they have serious pelvic pain, or 10 years later, when they can't get pregnant, that they had this STD that would have been easily curable."

STDs such as chlamydia, gonorrhea, syphilis, and trichomoniasis are nonviral and therefore curable if detected early enough. Other STDs, however, are viral and have no cure. These include HPV, genital herpes, sexually transmitted hepatitis B, and the human immunodeficiency virus, or HIV, which is responsible for 90,000 cases of AIDS annually, a figure that was dramatically expanded in 1993 over previous years due to an official redefinition of AIDS.

As many as 56 million individuals—more than one in five Americans—may be infected with an incurable viral STD other than AIDS.

STDs are "a tremendous problem," says W. David Hager, president of the Infectious Diseases Society for Obstetrics and Gynecology.

"Last fall [1997], a *New England Journal of Medicine* article found that slightly over 21 percent of Americans over age 12 are herpes simplex virus positive," Hager says. "That equals 45 million people."

"Furthermore, huge numbers of coeds on college campuses have HPV. Ninety-five percent of all cervical cancer and dysplasia [abnormal growth of organs or cells] are caused by HPV. And this may only be the tip of the iceberg."

The Institute of Medicine (IOM) estimates that the annual direct and indirect costs of selected major STDs, in addition to the human suffering associated with them, are approximately $10 billion. If sexually transmitted HIV infections are included, the total rises to $17 billion.

Medically, experts agree that the main risk factor for contracting an STD is promiscuity.

## The Perils of Promiscuity

"Having more than one lifetime sexual partner connotes risk," says Shepherd Smith, president of the Institute for Youth Development

(IYD). "The more partners, the more risk. It's that simple."

Compared with men and women who have had only 1 partner, those who report 2–3 partners are 5 times as likely to have had an STD; those with 4–6 lifetime partners are 10 times as likely; and the odds are 31 times greater for those who report 16 or more partners.

But Americans today are far more promiscuous than in the past. One big reason is that people are initiating sexual intercourse at younger ages, which usually leads to a higher number of partners during their lifetime.

According to a national poll of more than 11,000 high-school-aged youths, 54 percent said they were sexually active, compared with 29 percent in 1970. The proportion of 15-year-olds who have had sex has risen from 4.6 percent in 1970 to 26 percent. And almost one-fifth of the sexually active teens say they have had four or more partners.

In urban areas, the percentage of sexually experienced women aged 15–19 who reported four or more sex partners increased from 14 percent in 1971 to 31 percent in 1988.

"Sexual behavior is putting a sizable portion of high school students at risk," says Richard Lowry, an adolescent-health expert at the federal Centers for Disease Control and Prevention (CDC).

Having several partners is especially dangerous for teenage girls, he says, because studies show that they have often have an immature cervix, which may be more easily infected.

While experts agree that promiscuity is a major risk factor, liberals and conservatives generally hold very different values regarding promiscuity. Conservatives usually believe that promiscuity in and of itself is unhealthy and should be prevented by advocating abstinence until marriage and faithfulness within marriage.

Liberals usually argue that promiscuity already exists, that it results from legitimate personal choices, and that it is not necessarily something that can or should be prevented. Rather, people should be educated about their risks so that they can protect themselves with condoms if they choose to have more than one sexual partner.

## The Conservative Prevention Strategy

To conservatives, America's STD epidemic is really a problem of promiscuity, a symptom of society's moral decline, which began with the 1960s sexual revolution.

Joe McIlhaney, president of the Medical Institute for Sexual Health in Austin, Texas, says that "the reason there are more [sexually transmitted] diseases now than 30 years ago is because the ethics and values of society have changed."

There has been, he says, "a weakening of values, not just those having to do with sex, but also of other values like respect, responsibility, integrity." He says parents are not teaching their children these values strongly anymore.

Hager concurs. "Family breakdown and the loss of a great deal of family identity," he says, have contributed to a problem he's seeing become more common among young women: "A majority of young women that we see with STDs come from a situation where they are seeking the love and intimacy that they have missed in their homes."

To reverse the moral decline, conservatives advocate reinstating the traditional values of abstinence until marriage and faithfulness within marriage.

First, "parents should give unambiguous messages regarding appro priate sexual conduct," says the IYD's Smith.

Research shows that parents have the biggest impact of anyone on kids' behavior. And, according to the National Longitudinal Study on Adolescent Health, the largest-ever survey of American adolescents, kids were more likely to abstain from sex if their parents encouraged them to wait until marriage and discouraged birth control.

Kids also need to know that "sex within marriage is truly worth wait-ing for," Smith continues. "The NORC [National Opinion Research Center] study in Chicago found that the most sexually satisfied Ameri-cans are those who are in monogamous married relationships."

Second, "educators and medical professionals need to come around and help the parents to avoid disease and have a consistent message," says McIlhaney. He suggests that schools teach a character-based sex education program, because "values are the foundation on which good character is built."

"Young people will behave at the level of greatest expectation," says Hager. "If your expectation of young people is that they will engage in sexual activity, you aren't teaching them appropriate restraints.

"If your expectation of young people is that they can abstain, your educational program and expectations will give them enough hope that they will be able to abstain."

## The Liberal Prevention Strategy

Unlike conservatives, liberals think that preventing promiscuity is unrealistic and not even necessarily desirable.

Instead, they envision a culture where people are open and com-fortable with their sexuality so each person would be able to negotiate with his sexual partner about what he wants or doesn't want from sex. Preventing promiscuity, therefore, is not the goal; preventing unprotected intercourse is.

To liberals, the problem of high STD rates stems from Americans' inability to talk about sexuality and provide factual sex education in the home, school, and health care setting.

Peggy Clarke, president of the American Social Health Association, the only nongovernmental organization devoted to fighting STDs, says that the reason STDs are flourishing is that "we, as a culture, have not been good at dealing with sexuality."

"We need to raise people's skills in talking about sexuality and becoming more comfortable with it," says Kent Klindera, director of the HIV/STD education department at Advocates for Youth. The message that humans are "sexual beings" has to come from all sectors of society, he says, including "schools, churches, the mass media."

For example, Klindera conducts a peer education program through the Episcopal Church. His workshops help young people build better communication skills around their sexuality, whether it be through condom negotiation or abstinence role playing. He says if young people can communicate better about their sexuality, they'll be able to prevent the spread of STDs.

Liberals say that the best way to prevent STDs among the sexually active is to use condoms. They claim that condoms are "very effective" in preventing disease if used correctly every time. Thus, they want condoms to be distributed in schools, and they advocate increased funding for clinics that distribute condoms.

The AGI's Donovan says television networks should air condom ads to educate people about the risks of unprotected sex.

Planned Parenthood sums up the communication and condoms message this way: "Talk with your partners before the heat of passion, and use a condom every time!"

## The Values Battlefield

Conservatives say that the liberal approach is ultimately self-defeating, primarily because the underlying problem of promiscuity is not addressed. They also believe condoms are a poor substitute for true prevention, citing the following reasons:

1. Sending the implicit message that sex outside marriage is permissible will increase the number of people choosing to have sex with multiple partners.

2. Talking explicitly about sexuality piques curiosity and increases the likelihood of sexual experimentation.

3. Condoms provide only partial protection at best. Studies show that condoms have a 12–16 percent failure rate at preventing pregnancy after one year of using the devices. And while pregnancy can only occur a few days during the month, an STD can be transmitted any time a person has sex. Studies also indicate that condoms provide no detectable protection against HPV, genital herpes, or chlamydia.

4. It is unrealistic to expect people to use condoms consistently and correctly with every act of intercourse for a long period of time. McIlhaney says that the highest rate of condom use is a little more than 50 percent, and this was among adults who knew their partners were HIV-positive and whose participation in a research study exposed them to constant encouragement to use condoms. He also cites a 1997 CDC update that said that if people do not use condoms effectively 100 percent of the time, the outcome would be the same

as if they were not using condoms at all.

Liberals say that their approach is superior to the conservatives' for the following reasons:

1. Promiscuity exists, and a "just say no" message is an inadequate and unrealistic response. Conservatives have no response, liberals say, for those who choose to be sexually active outside marriage.

2. Condoms provide very effective protection against STDs. When asked about the 12–16 percent pregnancy failure rate of condoms, liberals respond that such a rate reflects "typical use." Perfect use of condoms, they say, results in an annual pregnancy rate of only 2 percent. They are also adamant about the effectiveness of condoms in preventing STDs. Planned Parenthood says that latex condoms offer "good protection" against many STDs, including gonorrhea, HIV, syphilis, and chancroid, and "some protection" against HPV and genital herpes.

3. Their approach does not impose moral absolutes on people's sexual behavior. Choosing abstinence is just as fine an option as choosing to be sexually active using condoms. It is more important that people be open and comfortable with their own sexuality.

In the final analysis, liberals are right in saying that not everyone is going to practice abstinence until marriage and faithfulness within marriage.

Conservatives are also accurate in saying that far from everyone who engages in sex with multiple partners is going to use condoms consistently and correctly 100 percent of the time.

But ultimately, the debate is more about values than science. It's about whose ideas about human sexuality, family, and lifestyle will prevail.

And that is a question only the American public can answer.

# CONDOMS OFFER PROTECTION AGAINST STDS

Willard Cates Jr.

A report issued by the National Institutes of Health (NIH) on the effectiveness of condoms in protecting against the spread of sexually transmitted diseases (STDs) cautioned against misinterpretation, but advocates on both sides of the condom debate used the report's results to bolster their positions, writes Willard Cates Jr. in the following selection. Condom supporters claim that the report underestimated condoms' effectiveness, while opponents claimed that the report proved the ineffectiveness of condoms in preventing the transmission of STDs. According to Cates, however, the report indicates that when used properly, condoms do protect against STDs. For example, condoms are effective against the most serious STD, HIV, and the most easily transmitted, gonorrhea and chlamydia. Cates concedes that condoms do not work perfectly, but to dismiss their use because they are not foolproof denies many people the opportunity to protect themselves. Cates is president of Family Health International, in Research Triangle Park, North Carolina.

On July 20, 2001, the National Institutes of Health (NIH) released its long-awaited report on condom effectiveness. This report summarized a workshop held more than 13 months previously, in June 2000, to evaluate the scientific evidence on condom effectiveness for preventing sexually transmitted infections (STIs). While both the workshop and the report were generally modeled on the NIH consensus conference approach, the effort had originated as a result of a congressional request, and thus had both a political and a scientific agenda. This tension between politics and science affected not only the origins of this report, but also its processes along the way and its interpretation after it was released.

## Preparing the Report

Although NIH was responsible for overseeing the workshop and finalizing the report, three other U.S. agencies participated in organizing

From "The NIH Condom Report: The Glass Is 90% Full," by Willard Cates Jr., *Family Perspectives*, September/October 2001. Copyright © 2001 by the Alan Guttmacher Institute. Reprinted with permission.

the review—the Centers for Disease Control and Prevention (CDC), the U.S. Food and Drug Administration (FDA) and the U.S. Agency for International Development (USAID). Each agency brought its own perspective to the table. The NIH provided its focus on molecular and clinical research, the CDC its expertise in epidemiology and prevention, the FDA its interests in product quality and labeling, and USAID its concerns for preventing the spread of STIs and HIV worldwide. The U.S. government representatives formed a Steering Committee for the workshop. In addition, a panel of 28 people was chosen from a spectrum of backgrounds and ideologies to help craft the report. The workshop itself was attended by 180 interested individuals.

The ground rules for the report were made clear from the outset. The panel examined only those peer-reviewed, published articles included in the presentations at the workshop. This limitation ensured that the independent scientific evaluation that occurs prior to publication was inherent in all of the data considered. While this approach allowed a certain quality control, it meant that several bodies of data (e.g., those available but unpublished, or those published but deemed unacceptable by the speakers) were not included in the full set of information considered by the panel. Nonetheless, an impressive array of 138 peer-reviewed articles that had been published by the time of the workshop were the basis for the NIH report.

The report was limited to evaluating the effectiveness of male latex condoms used during penile-vaginal intercourse. It examined evidence on eight STIs—HIV, gonorrhea, chlamydia, syphilis, chancroid, trichomoniasis, genital herpes and genital human papillomavirus. The evaluation methodology was extensive, considering both the efficacy (ideal use) and the effectiveness (typical use) of the condom. The quality of the study design, the ascertainment of exposure (e.g., consistent condom use), the laboratory measures of outcome (e.g., STIs) and the adequacy of statistical analytic approaches were examined.

## Drawing Conclusions

Several main conclusions emerged from the report:

• *Condom quality.* The available male latex condoms are of high quality. Studies based on viral penetration assays have shown condoms to provide a "highly effective barrier to transmission of particles of similar size to those of the smallest [sexually transmitted disease (STD)] viruses."

• *Condom trends.* During the 1980s and 1990s, condom use increased in the United States at the same time that HIV prevention efforts were stepped up. Moreover, the groups in which condom use increased most rapidly are those at greatest risk for STIs—adolescents, young adults and ethnic minorities.

• *Condom failures.* Condom breakage and slippage occurs in an estimated 1.6–3.6% of coital acts. These events are related to user experience with condoms. However, the most important factor affecting condom failure is *nonuse* of the method, rather than breakage or slippage.

• *Condom effectiveness.* Adequate data are available to conclude that consistent and correct condom use prevents unintended pregnancies, HIV infection and gonorrhea in men. Evidence that condom use prevents the other six STIs reviewed by the panel is insufficient, however.

• *Quality of evidence.* The report emphasized that "the absence of definitive conclusions reflected inadequacies of the evidence available and should not be interpreted as proof of the adequacy or inadequacy of the condom to reduce the risk of STDs other than HIV transmission in men and women and gonorrhea in men." All studies reviewed by the panel were observational in nature and carry a variety of methodological limitations well described in the text.

Unfortunately, as the report states, it is not possible to evaluate condom effectiveness using the ideal study design—a prospective, randomized controlled trial. In populations at high risk for STIs, for ethical reasons individuals cannot be randomized to a group that is not to use condoms. In and of itself, this situation speaks to the acceptance of condom effectiveness as the ethical standard of care within the scientific and clinical communities.

## Evaluating Additional Developments

Between the workshop of June 2000 and the report of July 2001, several events pertinent to its conclusions occurred. In September 2000, CDC convened an expert panel to review its STD Treatment Guidelines. In February 2001, USAID held an open forum to examine the topic of promoting condoms for dual protection against unintended pregnancy and STIs. Finally, on July 5, 2001, responding to the Public Law 106-554 requirement to provide "medically accurate information regarding the effectiveness or lack of effectiveness of condoms in preventing [STDs]," CDC issued a set of "prevention messages" to state health departments and its other grantees. The conclusions of the documents from all three groups were the same—namely, that "correct and consistent use of latex condoms can reduce the risk of [STIs]."

These conclusions were supported both by supplementary data not considered by the panel and by additional literature not covered in the report. For example, four studies not included in the chlamydia section of the report demonstrated that condom use has a protective effect against chlamydia among women; likewise, two studies implied that condoms protected against chlamydia in men. For gonorrhea, a similar situation existed regarding the condom's protective effect among women. Finally, for genital herpes, a recently published study of couples in which one member was infected with herpes simplex virus type 2 and the other was not found that condom use was associated with protection against infection among women. Therefore, this additional scientific literature supports even stronger statements than those contained in the NIH report about the condom's effectiveness against other STIs.

In addition, on August 16, 2001, the United Nations Joint Programme on HIV/AIDS and the World Health Organization issued a statement emphasizing the importance of condoms as "the best defense" in preventing STIs. These organizations underscored the global imperative to continue promoting condoms for HIV prevention. They also worried that contrasting interpretations could detract from efforts to halt HIV spread.

Finally, Thailand provides a real-world example of the condom's effectiveness in stemming the spread of STIs and HIV. In 1991, the Thai government implemented a "100% condom program" to encourage widespread condom use in commercial sex facilities. The proportion of commercial sex acts in which condoms were used increased from a reported 25% in 1989 to 94% in 1995. During the same interval, the incidence of curable STIs reported from government clinics decreased dramatically. Moreover, HIV prevalence among Thai military recruits also decreased.

Thus, whether for individual clinicians counseling clients about their personal risks or for policymakers deciding on the relative value of emphasizing condom use as part of an STI and HIV prevention strategy, the data are compelling: Condoms *do* protect against STIs and HIV, and are most effective when used consistently and correctly.

## Interpreting the Report

The response to the report was immediate and polarized. A group of physicians held a press conference to proclaim that the report demonstrated the ineffectiveness of condom use. These advocates saw themselves as exposing the "fact that condoms are ineffective in preventing transmission of most STDs, thus challenging the notion of 'safe sex' as championed by the CDC." Unfortunately, by inferring that absence of data meant condom ineffectiveness, the group did exactly what the report cautioned readers not to do. The group went even further in calling for the resignation of CDC director Jeffrey Koplan, alleging that his agency had "deliberately misrepresented condom effectiveness." Moreover, they implied the only reason the report had been released was that they had filed a Freedom of Information Act request.

On the other side, some congressional representatives criticized the report for its "misleading statements regarding the effectiveness of condoms." These politicians felt that the report understated the strong epidemiologic evidence supporting the effectiveness of condoms against such infections as chlamydia, gonorrhea, trichomoniasis and genital herpes. Stating that the report was flawed and undermined public confidence in condoms, they feared that this could lead to "decreases in condom use and increases in risky behavior, and the spread of [STIs]." The representatives called for an independent review of the scientific evidence by the Institute of Medicine.

Even press headlines reflected the dichotomy of opinion. CNN, the first news service to break the report, proclaimed "Condom report questions STD protection" on its website. However, the Associated Press declared, "Condoms protect against HIV, gonorrhea." A variety of follow-up articles expressed clinicians' concern about the report's being misinterpreted, although both sides had generated their own spin.

## The Take-Home Messages

First, the report itself was a quality effort. The NIH and the other federal agencies did their assigned job by reviewing and summarizing the available scientific evidence. The main problem was timeliness, caused in part by multiple reviews to accommodate sensitivities to political misinterpretation.

Second, from a public health perspective, the data clearly show that the glass is 90% full (that condoms are relatively effective) and only 10% empty (that data are inadequate). Male condom mechanics and quality assurance are good; moreover, levels of condom breakage and slippage are low and are not a major public health problem. At both the individual and the population levels, nonuse of male condoms is the predominant factor affecting condom failure. Because trends in condom use among the highest-risk populations have been encouraging, interpretations of the data that would discourage condom use might enhance the spread of STIs.

Third, existing studies demonstrate that the effectiveness of male condoms varies by the particular STI. In part, this is what I call the condom's "forgiveness factor"—namely, its ability to withstand certain levels of inconsistent use without allowing transmission of an infection (or permitting a pregnancy). This forgiveness measure is directly related to the organism's "beta"—its ability to be transmitted during a single act of unprotected intercourse. In general, the lower the beta, the higher the forgiveness with imperfect use. HIV is less easily transmitted and gonorrhea is more easily transmitted during unprotected coitus; thus, the condom is more forgiving of imperfect use when it comes to HIV prevention than it is for gonorrhea prevention.

Fourth, the inadequacy of the data should not be interpreted as indicating the inadequacy of condoms. Deliberate attempts to characterize the evidence as demonstrating the "ineffectiveness of condoms" constitute a misunderstanding of what the report states. Moreover, such misrepresentation can undermine the public's confidence in condoms, thereby leading to nonuse and to further spread of STIs and HIV.

## The Next Steps

The data presented in the report, as well as subsequent evidence available since the workshop, are clear. Male latex condoms are effective in preventing the most serious STI (HIV), the most easily transmitted

STIs (gonorrhea and chlamydia) and another important sexually transmitted condition (unplanned pregnancy). A crucial qualifier to this statement is that condoms work best when they are used consistently and correctly. All public health messages must reinforce the notion of condom effectiveness. The goal is to increase levels of consistent and correct male condom use in sexually active populations with a high prevalence of STIs and HIV.

Having emphasized that condoms work, we must also realize they do not work perfectly. But nothing in medicine (or in life, for that matter) always works. A full decade before the hoopla generated by this report, absolutist approaches to HIV prevention were being demanded: In 1991, an article in a national periodical was entitled "There is no safe sex." The author argued that because condoms were not foolproof in preventing HIV infection, the combination of abstaining from sex until marriage and practicing monogamy thereafter provided our only hope against the further spread of HIV. This is the same recommendation being made today by the physician advocacy group.

We must not, in Voltaire's terms, let "the best be the enemy of the good." Our prevention approaches—not only to HIV, but to other conditions as well—recognize that incremental, partially effective steps are necessary to mount collectively effective (but imperfect) prevention programs. The aggregation of these combination prevention strategies can have a dramatic effect on HIV spread.

The STI and HIV epidemics are not monolithic events that happen in the same way or at the same rate in all groups. They are not uniformly susceptible to claims of panacea-prone advocates. Controlling the spread of STIs will require different, mutually reinforcing techniques to reach the myriad of groups in our pluralistic society. The NIH condom report shows that male latex condoms are effective interventions that help to prevent the spread of STIs and unintended pregnancy. They must be the mainstay of our dual protection strategies both in the United States and globally. Any attempt to undermine their use will have a negative and long-lasting public health impact.

# CONDOMS DO NOT PROTECT AGAINST STDS

*Medical Letter on the CDC & FDA*

In the following selection, the editors of the *Medical Letter on the CDC & FDA* discuss a report issued by the National Institutes of Health (NIH) on the effectiveness of condoms in preventing the transmission of sexually transmitted diseases (STDs). The report, the authors observe, indicates that condoms are not effective in preventing all STDs. The Physicians Consortium, a group of doctors who advocate sound public health policy, claims that the report supports their position that condoms do not provide safe sex and that policies that advocate condom use are dangerous. The physicians' group emphasizes, for example, that condoms do not protect against three of the most prevalent diseases—chlamydia, genital herpes, and human papillomavirus. However, the authors write, the consortium fears that monetary investment in the message that condoms prevent STDs may keep the public from hearing the truth. The *Medical Letter on the CDC & FDA* is a publication of NewsRx, which provides businesses and consumers with news on health issues.

Condoms, long the mainstay of the "safe-sex" public health model, do not protect against the spread of nearly all sexually transmitted diseases. This is the major finding of a benchmark report released on Friday by the U.S. Department of Health and Human Services (HHS).

"Clinical research and experience has long caused us to seriously doubt the effectiveness of condoms to provide 'safe sex,'" said Dr. Hal Wallis, a spokesman for the Physicians Consortium, a group of more than 2,000 doctors who advocate for sound public health policy. "I am shocked to see the conclusions of the paper so candidly confirm this suspicion to the degree that it does. The clinical evidence is now clear: condoms do not offer 'safe sex.' The entire public health model developed by the CDC, and based on the idea that condoms offer protection, is a lie. The skeleton is now out of the closet," Wallis added.

Wallis, an OB/GYN from Texas, said that his practice is increasingly

From "NIH Report Shows That Condoms Do Not Provide Safe Sex," *Medical Letter on the CDC & FDA*, July 20, 2001.

devoted to HPV-infected women, many of whom have developed cervical cancer. HPV [human papillomavirus] is the cause of nearly all cases of cervical cancer and is also linked to oral, anal and prostate cancer. But, according to Wallis, "The CDC has placed all of its eggs in the AIDS basket, which truly is a major health threat, but has done so at the expense of all other STDs." Nearly 5,000 women die from the disease every year. Cervical cancer has claimed the lives of more women in the U.S. than has AIDS.

The study did not find proof that condoms protect against the three most prevalent STDs, chlamydia, genital herpes and HPV. "These three STDs infect 9 million people per year," said Dr. John Diggs, another spokesman for the physicians group. "More than 60 million Americans suffer from these three diseases, and the CDC won't even tell them the truth about condoms," Diggs added.

During the past year, a panel comprised of the Food and Drug Administration (FDA), National Institutes of Health (NIH), the Centers for Disease Control and Prevention (CDC), the U.S. Agency for International Development (USAID) and non-governmental consultants studied all the available clinical and peer-reviewed research on the effectiveness of condoms to prevent the spread of STDs.

The panel examined eight STDs: HIV/AIDS, chancroid, genital herpes, human papillomavirus, gonorrhea, syphilis, trichomoniasis and chlamydia. The panel found that the correct and consistent use of condoms reduced the risk of HIV by 85 percent and could reduce the risk of gonorrhea, but only among men. (Yet, numerous research studies indicate that the vast majority of sexually active people, especially teenagers, are either unable or unwilling to use condoms correctly and consistently.) The panel found no clinical evidence that condoms were effective at all against any of the other STDs studied.

The Physicians Consortium is concerned that the public health service might not be willing to set the record straight. "Condom packaging and most educational materials and Web sites promoting 'safe sex' continue to make the claim that condoms are 98 percent effective against HIV/AIDS and other STDs. It is now clear that all of this material must be revised to reflect the facts," Wallis said.

Diggs concluded, "The safe-sex message is a billion dollar business. Many federal agencies and contractors will face financial hardship if they start acknowledging the truth. It will be interesting to see if money will outweigh the chance to be honest."

The Physicians Consortium represents more than 2,000 medical doctors and healthcare professionals dedicated to bringing evidence-based science into public health policy.

# Abstinence Education Can Prevent STDs in Adolescents

Catherine Edwards

Arguing that condoms do not protect against some of the most insidious sexually transmitted diseases (STDs) such as the human papillomavirus, some authorities contend that abstinence education is the only answer to preventing the spread of STDs among adolescents, writes Catherine Edwards in the following selection. To help teen girls avoid STDs and unwanted pregnancies, one such program, known as Best Friends, encourages girls to abstain from sex until marriage, says Edwards. The Best Friends program begins in elementary school and continues through high school and not only encourages abstinence but promotes self-esteem and educates participants on the dangers of STDs. According to the author, while authorities assert that some programs have wasted federal funds slated for abstinence education, the privately funded Best Friends program is considered a success: Graduates were less likely to have had sex than adolescents who had not been through the program. Edwards is a staff writer for *Insight on the News*, a national weekly news magazine.

Penn State University Freshman Lesley Long knew what to tell the young man who kept knocking on her door and coming in to sit on her dorm-room bed. "Look, I don't want to have sex with you," she said directly, taking him completely off guard. "I'm a virgin and am waiting until I am married. Now go away!" In disbelief the young man pressed her on the issue until, shrugging and with a sheepish grin, he realized she meant what she said.

## Getting the Message Early

Long had been a member of an "abstinence only" education program, called "Best Friends," in her Washington public school since she was 12 years old. Best Friends is a program for girls that begins in elementary school and continues through graduation from high school. It teaches teen-agers to abstain from sex, drugs and alcohol. The girls participate in an instructional curriculum throughout the year, engage in group discussion and work with mentors at their schools to help keep them accountable to their commitment. They learn the benefits of exercise and good nutrition and the dangers of HIV/AIDS and other sexually transmitted diseases (STDs).

"This kind of education requires long-term commitment and we get results," says Best Friends board member Mary Jane Shackelford. "But we have to start with girls as early as the fifth grade now." On a cool July 2001 morning, Lesley Long and Maria Bennett—two girls who have been graduated from the program—sat down with *Insight* to explain why abstinence-only education works. As Bennett put it, "A lot of guys respect you more when they know you respect yourself enough to wait until marriage to have sex. Best Friends gives you confidence. It's not just about sex; it's about being smart and making wise decisions."

Bennett will attend Hofstra University in the fall of 2001. She and Long both have received scholarships from Best Friends to help fund their university education.

The girls say they are amazed by the lack of knowledge other teens have about STDs. "See, Best Friends doesn't just say, 'Don't have sex,'" Bennett explains. "They say why you shouldn't and then also tell us about all the diseases you can get. I am amazed that most kids know nothing about even the most common diseases out there."

Bennett's observations are echoed by many lawmakers and other public officials who believe that teens are not being given the proper message about sex, even as a public-health issue, and that there is no such thing as "safe sex." Best Friends receives no federal funding, but has proved more effective than other abstinence-based programs.

## Promoting Abstinence

In 1996, Congress mandated that $50 million be set aside as direct block grants to states to promote abstinence education among the young. Much of the money was wasted, say congressional staffers, but $20 million more now has been appropriated and this time programs and expenditures will be monitored closely by Congress.

In Utah, for example, much of the money was spent on recreation programs and field trips, including $800 for basketballs and soccer equipment. In Montana, as much as 78 percent of its federal funding for abstinence education was spent on administrative overhead despite the fact that federal regulations have put a 10 percent cap on overhead.

Rep. Ernest Istook, R-Okla., sits on the House Appropriations Committee, and his staff tells *Insight* he will monitor spending personally on this program to ensure tax money is spent as Congress intended. In 2000, Istook confronted the Clinton administration for trying to cut abstinence funding from the budget. The congressman said then,

"It's sad that the Clinton administration condones the teen sex that causes disease, unwanted pregnancies and abortions and that traps young mothers in a cycle of poverty. I won't give up on my effort to help our youth avoid this, and neither will the Congress."

Why this movement of the issue from one of morality to one of public health? Is the latter just more politically correct than the former, or has widespread sexual promiscuity created unprecedented dangers? The deadly threat of HIV/AIDS is well-known. But, contrary to popular belief, the most common sexually transmitted diseases cannot reliably be prevented by wearing a condom. Human papilloma virus (HPV), the most common STD, is one of them. It causes more than 90 percent of cancer and pre-cancer of the cervix, which is in turn the cause of more than 5,000 deaths of American women per year. According to a report issued by the surgeon general, 5.5 million new cases of cervical cancer are occurring per year.

Meanwhile, there are 12 million new cases of STDs annually, and 22 percent of all Americans age 12 and older have been infected with genital herpes, an incurable venereal disease that wearing a condom does not prevent. Among African-American girls older than age 11, the incidence is pandemic, with 49 percent suffering genital herpes. The most commonly reported STD among all American women is chlamydia—which is the cause of infertility in one-third of women of child-bearing age who cannot become pregnant.

## The Risk of Promoting Condoms Alone

This alarms former Rep. Tom Coburn, R-Okla., who is a medical doctor. Coburn introduced a law that was passed and signed by President Clinton in December 2000 mandating that the Centers for Disease Control and Prevention (CDC) immediately start warning the public that condoms do not prevent HPV and subsequent cancer. The House Government Reform and Oversight Committee has been sending letters to the CDC complaining about failure to comply. "The message that there is such a thing as 'safe sex' and all will be well if kids use a condom is a myth," says Coburn, who since retiring from Congress has returned to his obstetrics practice in Oklahoma. "When I was in medical school there were two of these diseases: syphilis and gonorrhea," he adds. "Since then the number of STDs has exploded."

Coburn is concerned that groups promoting condom use might be able to prevent some HIV cases, but they ignore the other STDs. "Abstinence is the only answer," he tells *Insight*. "I think by giving any other message to our kids we sell them short. We expect kids to abstain from drugs, tell them so, and we believe in their ability to do it. Same with drinking and smoking. Why not with sex? If we don't we are sending a mixed message."

Joe McIlhaney, a physician, is president of the Medical Institute on Sexual Health, a Texas-based nonprofit health-education organization. According to McIlhaney, "We have to educate our kids to the consequences of not remaining abstinent. Unfortunately some of the worst educated are church groups who know to remain abstinent but know nothing of the health risks involved in sexual activity."

U.S. Surgeon General David Satcher released a controversial report at the end of June 2001 titled, *A Call to Action to Promote Sexual Health and Responsible Sexual Behavior.* "I applaud the surgeon general on some of his findings—especially that we cannot stand by and do nothing," says Elayne Bennett, founder of the Best Friends Foundation, who adds: "We must do something." But while Bennett approves of the surgeon general's promotion of youth-development programs to teach young people about responsible behavior in a time of pandemic STD infection, she is concerned that the report fails to encourage abstinence before marriage. "In educating our kids we sell them short by telling them only about how to have safe sex and not telling them the great benefits of commitment and marriage. It is irresponsible not to do so."

## The Long-Term Goals

Which is why Best Friends focuses on the whole person, not just their sexuality. "It might take a few years to really get the message across to a kid to abstain from sex," says George Sanker, program director for Best Men, a pilot program for boys modeled after Best Friends. "But kids need role models and peer groups as well as a good curriculum to help them abstain from sex. A few classes are just not enough. And they need positive role models monitoring them and who can be there for them when they run into trouble or peer pressure."

As Long remembers it, "In junior high they told us, 'You should wait because you are special.' Well I sort of believed them, but when I got to high school and was older I could understand more and fully understood the reasons I should stick to these decisions. But it took a few years!"

Of course, Best Friends does not shy away from educating about STDs; it just promotes abstinence as the only safe, responsible alternative to becoming a victim of the growing epidemics. How well is it working? In 1999, an independent researcher compared data about the behavior and attitudes of Washington public-school students with similar data collected from Best Friends girls attending those schools. The result is something to think about, say observers:

In Washington, 17.8 percent of seventh-grade girls and 32.8 percent of eighth-grade girls had engaged in sexual intercourse. The survey of Best Friends girls attending those same public schools found that only 4.2 percent of seventh-graders and 5.6 percent of eighth-graders had experienced sexual intercourse.

# THE RELATIONSHIP BETWEEN BEER TAXES AND GONORRHEA RATES

Ken Ringle

A Centers for Disease Control and Prevention (CDC) report issued in April 2000 estimates that a 20-cent increase in state beer taxes could reduce the rate of gonorrhea by nearly 9 percent, reports *Washington Post* staff writer Ken Ringle in the following selection. However, the statistics upon which this report is based, Ringle writes, have limitations that even the CDC acknowledges. Ringle contends that the statistics do not prove a causal relationship between higher beer taxes and gonorrhea rates.

As every genuine yuppie will tell you ad nauseam, obscure, expensive microbrews are vastly better than Budweiser. But did you realize cheap beer gives you gonorrhea?

If this loony assertion has somehow escaped you, you've failed to absorb the full implications of the latest study from the Sky Is Falling School of Scientific Statistics, which this week appears to have settled at the government's Centers for Disease Control and Prevention (CDC) in Atlanta.

On Thursday, April 27, 2000, the CDC—which normally knows better—released a report of a national study of alcohol policy changes from 1981 to 1995 headlined "Gonorrhea Rates Decline with Higher Beer Tax."

"CDC researchers," the department's summary of the report says, "estimate that a 20-cent state tax increase per six-pack of beer could reduce U.S. gonorrhea rates by almost 9 per cent." Gonorrhea is one of the most common sexually transmitted diseases.

## Questioning the Statistics

Hundreds of newspaper and broadcasting outlets, including *The Washington Post*, ran stories about the study without questioning its basic premise. That premise, says David Murray of the Statistical Assessment Service, is akin to saying "the sun goes down because we turn on the street lights."

Murray, whose Washington-based group attempts the impossible job of watchdogging fraudulent statistics in science and government, says given the amount of disposable income Americans have on hand, "the idea that you could reduce even unprotected sex, much less disease, with a 20-cent increase in the price of a six-pack is so wildly improbable as to be ludicrous."

But he says the study is a perfect example of how real science is increasingly taking a back seat to the mining and tweaking of statistics to further a political agenda.

"I'm not sure what the agenda is here," he says. "Maybe we're getting ready to sue Seagram's to cover the cost of treating sexual diseases."

But he pointed out that the four-page study has all the ingredients to stoke a major media feeding frenzy—sex, youth and alcohol.

Plus, of course, a potential corporate or governmental scapegoat for whoops-I-guess-I-shouldn't-have-done-that behavior.

Cynthia Glocker, media spokesman for the CDC's sexually transmitted disease division, says radio and television journalists across the country have flooded her office with requests for information and interviews.

## Acknowledging the Limitations

More than a few appeared to be skeptical of its findings, as, indeed, the CDC's own editors apparently are. Though the report seems to suggest a causal relationship between higher beer prices and lower gonorrhea rates among 15-to-19-year-olds in 24 out of 36 states, an editorial note accompanying the report says its findings are subject to "at least two limitations."

First, because state gonorrhea reporting practices vary, state-specific gonorrhea rates should be compared with caution. Second, the analysis may be subject to confounding effects of unobservable factors. . . . Omitting these variables could cause substantial bias."

Well, yes. Variables like the intelligence of the young people involved, the intensity of the beer party, the hygiene practices of the participants, their income level and whether they're swiping the beer from their parents' cooler.

"Given these limitations, the study findings . . . are consistent with but do not prove a causal relation between higher taxes and declining STD rates," the editorial note said.

So what's the point of the study?

"The study findings are consistent with the idea that higher taxes can reduce STD rates," says Harrell Chesson, a health economist with the CDC.

"The simplicity of this approach is that we don't look at the individual factors that might affect the relationship between alcohol consumption and risky sex. Alcohol use has been shown to be associated with risky sexual behavior. . . . All we look at is the relationship between alcohol policy and STD rates. . . . We said higher taxes could reduce the rate. We didn't say they would."

But if the government's alcohol policy is related to sexual behavior, how does he explain the nation's experiment with Prohibition in the 1920s? That touched off the greatest outbreak of alcohol consumption and uncontrolled sex seen in the nation until then.

"Our study didn't address Prohibition," Chesson says, sounding amused. "I don't know."

# USING THE INTERNET TO PREVENT THE SPREAD OF STDs

Lee Condon

According to Lee Condon, the San Francisco Stop AIDS Project instituted a chat room program designed to combat an outbreak of syphilis, and the program became a model for other Internet programs. Research reveals that those who use the Internet to find sex partners are more likely to have a history of sexually transmitted diseases (STDs), writes Condon. Armed with this information, the program's staff members enter chat rooms and field questions about STDs. Although the program's success is difficult to measure, the response has been positive. Condon is a contributing writer for the *Advocate*, a national gay and lesbian news magazine.

As the Internet has become more of a sexual playground for many gay men, it's also become a breeding ground for sexually transmitted diseases.

Now health educators, who used to spend countless hours doing street outreach, are logging on to the information superhighway instead. In fact, Marcel Miranda, a deputy program director at San Francisco's Stop AIDS Project, says he is more likely to be juggling instant messages about STDs on America Online than passing out condoms in the Castro [an area of San Francisco known for its large gay population].

## Answering Questions in Chat Rooms

Miranda, who uses the screen name StopAIDSMM, says he started entering sex chat rooms in March 2000, as a representative of Stop AIDS after health officials linked a spike in local syphilis cases to an AOL chat room in 1999. He created an AOL profile that announced he was available to answer questions about HIV and AIDS. Then he jumped into a chat room and waited for men to come to him.

"People in San Francisco know us. They know our name. I would let men come to me, and invariably I would get questions," Miranda says. "The anonymity lends itself to honest communication, espe-

From "Cruising for Safe Sex," by Lee Condon, *Advocate*, March 12, 2001. Copyright © 2001 by Capital City Press. Reprinted with permission.

cially for people who are closeted and questioning."

The experiment was so successful that Stop AIDS applied for a grant to start a regular program. Stop AIDS has been awarded a 15-month $135,000 contract with the San Francisco Department of Public Health. The goal is to have staff members and volunteers chat online with 300 to 400 men a month. Miranda says he has received inquiries about the program from around the country. Marty Algaze, the spokesman for Gay Men's Health Crisis in New York City, says members of the organization have talked about adding an Internet chat component to that agency's outreach efforts.

Another group that has followed Stop AIDS's lead is the Los Angeles County Department of Public Health, which used the chat program as part of its $500,000 effort to stop a syphilis outbreak there. Mark Caffee, a spokesman for the chat room program, says online chatters were very responsive. "We were there at the point when they were looking for a hookup," Caffee says. "We used the chat rooms as a way to be there when sex was on the brain."

Harlan Rotblatt, director of adolescent services for Los Angeles County's Sexually Transmitted Diseases Program, says the department was able to institute the chat room program because of an emergency allowance it was given to fight the outbreak. "Certainly, when you are dealing with a spreading disease, this worked great," Rotblatt says. Now that the outbreak is over and the money is gone, he doubts the health department will continue the program. However, he expects other agencies or nonprofits may use the pilot program as a model. "All you need is an Internet account to do this," he says.

Online educators in Los Angeles used a different strategy than the one employed by Stop AIDS. Instead of waiting for people to instant-message them, two online educators entered a chat room and started writing to each other about syphilis, using a scripted conversation. While there was some debate over whether it was appropriate to start fake conversations, ultimately health officials decided the strategy fit the culture of chat rooms.

"We were just using the regular rules of the chat room," Rotblatt says. Health officials, he says, wanted to avoid a heavy-handed approach such as going into chat rooms and making proclamations.

## Studying the Impact of the Internet

In 2000 the U.S. Centers for Disease Control and Prevention studied the risk of getting HIV and STDs from an online hookup. In one survey of adults at an HIV counseling and test center, researchers found that 16% of the respondents had used the Internet to find sex partners; most of these people had a greater likelihood of an STD history and more sexual partners than average adults. Future studies will explore the success potential of online prevention efforts.

Researchers also note that health officials have had success in reaching out to Internet sex surfers. Specifically, they say, the Internet has provided an easy means for officials to alert people to occurrences such as the syphilis outbreaks in San Francisco and Los Angeles.

Robert Kohn, an epidemiologist at the San Francisco Department of Public Health, says coping with the 1999 rash of syphilis cases in that city served as the starting point for the agency's Internet-related endeavors. Since then the department has conducted regular outreach efforts on Gay.com and PlanetOut, including the posting of information about STDs and HIV transmission. However, Kohn says, "it's impossible to say who reads that and what effect it has on people." It is also impossible to know how much impact Internet outreach has in stemming outbreaks.

Multicity studies currently under way, Kohn says, are taking a more comprehensive look at the spread of HIV and other STDs from sex that is initiated in chat rooms. "All it takes is one little contamination in that pool," Kohn says. "You don't know how big that pool is until you drain it."

## Making Contact

As a Web surfer in his personal life, Miranda says he knew how to position himself online to get "lurkers" to contact him. "There's very little chat going on," he says. "Everything tends to happen through instant messages. Online there are lurkers who check out the profiles of guys inside the rooms."

The Stop AIDS profiles include key words like "butt sex," "partying," "raw sex," "barebacking," and "safe sex." That way, if Internet users type in those words, a Stop AIDS profile will be one of the hits they get. Typical Stop AIDS profiles include lines like "Instant-message me if you'd like to talk about butt sex, raw sex, sucking, partying with crystal, HIV, condoms, where to meet guys."

Miranda says the organization makes a point of avoiding clinical descriptions such as "anal insertive" or "oral receptive" when discussing sex. Instead, he says, "we give men permission to talk about sex."

So far, the response to their efforts has been overwhelmingly positive, Miranda says. Most people ask about HIV and oral sex, STDs, and the relation of sexual risk to drug usage, he says, adding that many conversations are in-depth. Often chatters are referred to health service providers.

"Sometimes it's very slow. Sometimes it's very busy," Miranda says. "Sometimes I will have to juggle three or four instant messages at a time. Luckily, I'm a fast typist."

# STAMPING OUT SYPHILIS

Kathleen Fackelmann

Although the incidence of syphilis has diminished, this sexually transmitted disease (STD) remains a threat in certain areas of the United States, writes Kathleen Fackelmann in the following selection. Syphilis has become even more serious because it increases the risk of contracting HIV, the author notes. Unfortunately, she reports, several barriers stand in the way of eradicating the disease. For example, because of the stigma associated with syphilis and STDs in general, people are reluctant to talk about ways to reduce their risk. According to the author, researchers are working on a vaccine that could eliminate this devastating disease. Kathleen Fackelmann writes on health issues for publications such as *Science News* and *USA Today.*

Federal health officials have targeted an age-old enemy: *Treponema pallidum,* the spiral bacterium that causes syphilis. U.S. health officials have declared war on syphilis before, but this time the battle may be winnable. The Scandinavian countries have already conquered the disease.

## A Smoldering Fire

In the July 17, 1998, *Science,* Michael E. St. Louis and Judith N. Wasserheit of the Centers for Disease Control and Prevention (CDC) in Atlanta argue that now is the time to eliminate syphilis from the United States. Although the disease has been beaten back to an all-time low of just 3.2 cases per 100,000 people, that statistic doesn't adequately convey the threat that syphilis still poses, the researchers say. In the late 1980s, the number of cases spiked to 20 cases per 100,000 people, and it could rise again.

A 1998 scientific advance promises to speed up the work on a vaccine. Public health workers, however, do not plan to wait for vaccine development. The currently low incidence of syphilis represents "a small window of opportunity that we cannot [afford to] lose," says Charlie Rabins, chief of the sexually transmitted disease section of the Illinois Department of Public Health in Springfield.

Like a forest fire that continues to smolder in a few isolated areas, syphilis remains a threat in the southeastern United States and some urban areas. CDC officials note that in 1997, just 31 U.S. counties reported more than 50 percent of all syphilis cases. If left unchecked, those pockets of disease could ignite a public health disaster.

"We're sitting on a potentially massive bonfire," St. Louis warns.

## The HIV Connection

In the 1940s and again in the 1960s, public health programs substantially reduced syphilis rates in the United States but failed to eliminate the disease. Untreated, syphilis can lead to fatal heart disease and brain damage. Now, the AIDS epidemic is lending additional urgency to defeating syphilis.

People with sexually transmitted diseases face a greater threat of contracting HIV, the virus that causes AIDS, says Edward W. Hook III, who studies sexually transmitted diseases at the University of Alabama at Birmingham. Infection with *T. pallidum* causes an ulcerlike sore, called a chancre, on the genitals. Because that wound can serve as a portal of entry or exit for HIV, someone infected with syphilis can more easily contract HIV infection and also readily pass the deadly virus on to another person.

Indeed, researchers have noticed a number of links between syphilis and HIV infection. For example, the outbreak of syphilis in the southeastern United States contributed to the spread of HIV in that region, according to CDC research.

"We now have evidence that HIV transmission, particularly heterosexual HIV transmission across the South and in a few large cities, essentially echoes the syphilis epidemic of the late 1980s and early 1990s," Wasserheit says.

A syphilis outbreak that hit Baltimore in 1995, and continues to spread, also shows deadly ties with HIV. People in inner-city Baltimore who have been diagnosed with syphilis have a one-in-five chance of being infected with HIV, says Jonathan M. Zenilman of Johns Hopkins Medical Institutions in Baltimore. That's about four times the incidence found even in the high-risk group of people treated in clinics for a variety of sexually transmitted diseases, he says.

Aside from the AIDS concern, researchers note that a pregnant woman infected with syphilis can pass the disease to her fetus. During the most recent syphilis epidemic, from 1987 to 1993, 3,000 U.S. infants were born with this disease per year. Babies with syphilis can die from the infection or suffer blindness or lifelong neurological problems, St. Louis says.

At first glance, syphilis seems like an ideal candidate for elimination. The spirochete that causes the disease lives only in humans. The relatively long incubation period means that public health workers have enough time to identify potentially infected sexual partners before symptoms appear and provide them with injections of penicillin or other antibiotics.

## The Barriers to Eliminating Syphilis

Although antibiotics cure the infection, public health experts remain cautious about their chances of abolishing syphilis in the United States. "The most important barriers to eliminating syphilis are not biomedical," Wasserheit says.

To appreciate the difficulty of the task, consider that most people don't even want to talk about syphilis, colloquially known as bad blood or the pox. "As a society, we have a hard time talking frankly and openly about sex," St. Louis says.

Many people in the United States regard syphilis as a moral—not a public health—issue. "There's a tendency to think that those who've acquired a sexually transmitted disease got what they deserved," St. Louis says.

"If you approach this as something that is incontrovertibly wrong, you've really erected barriers to conversation, to risk reduction, and to any sort of educational process," Hook adds.

That problem is compounded by a lack in the United States of physician training about syphilis, says John E. Toney, an infectious disease specialist at the University of South Florida College of Medicine in Tampa. Toney says medical schools don't generally put much emphasis on diagnosing sexually transmitted infections. In addition, physicians may be reluctant to bring up the possibility of such infections with patients, he says.

Moreover, policy discussions of syphilis in the United States remain under the shadow cast by the Tuskegee Study. That infamous government project, conducted from 1932 until 1972, withheld treatment from black men afflicted with syphilis in an attempt to research the natural course of the disease.

The Tuskegee study is widely acknowledged today as a model of unethical research. In 1997, President Bill Clinton apologized formally for the study, which was supervised and funded by the CDC.

"One result [of the study's unethical protocol] has been the crippling of syphilis research and prevention programs, in part because of shame, distrust, and lack of frank dialogue and leadership," St. Louis and Wasserheit say in their *Science* article.

## The Problem of Poverty

Further complicating the task of eliminating syphilis is its ties with poverty. Syphilis flourishes in communities that lack "the financial and social resources to provide people with basic health care," Wasserheit says.

"In our country, unfortunately, that frequently means minority communities," she adds. Syphilis currently affects a disproportionate number of African Americans in the United States. Rates of syphilis are 50 times higher among blacks than among whites.

"The proportion of people living in poverty is greater in the southeastern United States," where syphilis remains most problematic, Hook says.

Drastic reductions in public health funding may also help explain why some areas get hit with an explosion of syphilis.

Consider Baltimore. From 1993 to 1995, the number of syphilis cases there doubled. Public health officials described the outbreak in the March 1, 1996 *Morbidity and Mortality Weekly Report*. They blamed the epidemic on the escalating use of crack cocaine, the practice of exchanging sex for drugs, and the breakdown of the public health system.

The report notes that the number of city health workers charged with the notification of sex partners of infected people has declined from 14 to 8 during the syphilis epidemic.

An epidemic, like that in Baltimore, of this easily treatable disease is a "sentinel public health event," Wasserheit says. "It means that the system is not functioning adequately."

Indeed, parts of the United States resemble less developed countries when it comes to sexually transmitted diseases. "We have to begin to address the question of why sexually transmitted diseases are 5 to 15 times higher in our nation than in any other developed country on Earth," Hook says. "In Scandinavia, the only way that people get syphilis is by leaving their country," he says.

Hook looked at the scope of sexually transmitted diseases in the United States as part of a committee appointed by the National Academy of Sciences' Institute of Medicine in Washington, D.C. In a 1997 report, that group concluded that an effective national system for preventing sexually transmitted diseases does not exist in the United States. The report estimates the direct and indirect costs associated with sexually transmitted diseases other than HIV infection at about $10 billion a year. It called sexually transmitted diseases "hidden epidemics of tremendous health and economic consequences."

## The Hope of Genetic Research

A recent scientific advance may help pave the way toward CDC's goal of syphilis elimination. In July 1998, Claire M. Fraser of the Institute for Genomic Research in Rockville, Md., and her colleagues reported the genetic sequence of *T. pallidum*. With the blueprint for the molecular secrets of this bacterium in hand, researchers finally may be able to develop a vaccine against syphilis, Wasserheit says.

Scientists have been unable to create a vaccine in large part because they haven't found a way to culture *T. pallidum* in the laboratory. The spirochete can only be grown in mammals, usually rabbits, which makes it difficult to study, says St. Louis.

A vaccine for syphilis would go a long way toward stamping out the disease. "Public health disease eradication has never been successful without a vaccine," Hook says.

In addition to facilitating a vaccine, the genetic sequence of *T. pallidum* may also help medical investigators track a syphilis epidemic, St. Louis notes. Researchers could distinguish, or type, different strains of syphilis and use the information to trace an infection back to its origin. Now, investigators must ask each patient to recall recent sexual partners, a process that is often fraught with poor memory.

"You can almost never connect all the dots in these outbreaks," St. Louis says. With genetic typing, researchers might be able to quickly track an emerging syphilis flare-up, he says.

## The Time Is Right

Public health experts argue that there may never be a better time to launch a strike against syphilis. "In 1997, 85 percent of new syphilis cases were in just 6 percent of counties," says Wasserheit. "That means we can go in in a very targeted way and focus our efforts."

"CDC is demonstrating a level of commitment that hasn't been seen in the past," Hook says. Previously, he notes, funding was cut when the national syphilis rates dropped to low levels, an error that may have led to more outbreaks of this disease.

CDC is vowing to correct the mistakes of the past. The agency has proposed that Congress set aside $25 million per year for 5 years to help with the effort to erase syphilis.

Wasserheit notes that the federal government plays only one part in the campaign to achieve victory over *T. pallidum*. "At the federal level, we can try to help lead the charge, but the commitment will have to be at the state and local level," she says.

Baltimore is a case in point. "There has to be a serious commitment to looking at public health in this city," Zenilman says. "Eradication is not on the horizon here."

What happens if the move to quash syphilis in the U.S. fails? "The alternative to moving to elimination now is the resurgence of another epidemic of syphilis with its attendant consequences," Wasserheit says. History suggests that without a strong control program, syphilis breaks out every 7 to 10 years, Rabins adds.

"This disease is not going to sit still while we decide whether or not we really want to deliver a good knockout blow," Wasserheit says.

# WORKPLACE STRATEGIES TO COMBAT STDS

Helen Lippman

Employers are helping to pay for the costs associated with the treatment of STDs by providing health care benefits to their employees. Since the health care costs of sexually transmitted diseases (STDs) total more than 8 billion dollars annually, according to Helen Lippman, employers have a vested interest in addressing the STD epidemic. In the following selection, Lippman explains the benefits of preventative action. While the cost of screening is small, the author reports, the costs of treatment can be quite expensive, especially in view of the fact that STDs get worse over time. The author asserts, for example, that some STDs can lead to pelvic inflammatory disease (PID), which may go undetected until the disease travels to the fallopian tubes, resulting in ectopic pregnancies or infertility. According to the author, corporate strategies that remove the stigma of STDs and encourage screening can support both the health and economy of the workplace. Lippman is a contributing editor of *Business & Health*.

Forget the taboo. Sexually transmitted diseases (STDs) are costing American employers just as much as more socially acceptable medical conditions. A panel of experts from the public and private sectors suggests actions.

Although short-term disability is the only STD on most benefits managers' minds, the Washington Business Group on Health offered attendees at its 2001 conference a session on the ramifications of the other STD, sexually transmitted diseases.

## In the Dark

Highlighting the widespread ignorance about these diseases, Kathleen Toomey, director of the division of public health, Georgia Department of Human Resources—and one of the panelists at the conference session—recalled: "When I testified before the Georgia General Assembly about the scope and impact of sexually transmitted diseases, several legislators thought chlamydia was a flower being proposed to represent the state."

Lawmakers aren't the only ones in the dark. "Doctors often respond to questions about screening for STDs by insisting, 'This is not a problem for this community,' or 'for my patients,'" Toomey added.

Many employers echo the not-in-my-backyard cry. The conference session panelists, representing governmental and nonprofit public health agencies and corporate America, set out to debunk this and other myths.

## Making a Case for Employer Involvement

"STDs are very common in every community," Toomey declared. Ignoring them exacts a high price in terms of costly medical problems and productivity loss.

Direct medical costs for screening and treating sexually transmitted diseases total more than $8 billion annually, not counting HIV or AIDS. That total is roughly the same as the bill for asthma, a major focus of disease management and workplace programs.

Targeting management of STDs is far less common but offers a great return on investment, pointed out Roger Merrill, Perdue Farms' corporate medical director. "As a practical matter, women are getting Pap smears anyway. The cost of screening for other sexually transmit ted diseases is very small, early treatment is cheap and it's really expensive if you don't do it."

Underscoring just how widespread and serious the problem is, the speakers provided these statistics:

• One American in four will acquire an STD in the course of a lifetime;

• One in five has genital herpes, but 90 percent of those infected are not aware of it;

• More than 15 million people become infected every year, including about a third with human papilloma virus (HPV), the most common STD;

• Two thirds of those who get STDs are under 25, and the majority are women;

• At least 15 percent of female infertility problems stem from tubal damage caused by pelvic inflammatory disease (PID), the result of an untreated STD.

## The Impact on Women and Older Workers

"Sexually transmitted diseases disproportionately impact women," Toomey noted. "Although they're more likely to acquire STDs, they're less likely to realize they're infected," she added, and they're more apt to develop serious, sometimes life-threatening health problems as a result.

For instance, data shows that bacterial vaginosis can lead to premature delivery and infant mortality—and exorbitant costs. A single complicated delivery and newborn requiring intensive care can run up a tab of anywhere from $20,000 to more than $1 million, the March of Dimes reports.

Because young women face the greatest risk, employers with mostly older workers may assume there's no need for them to invest in what the Institute of Medicine has identified as a "hidden epidemic." But that's a faulty assumption, the panelists agreed.

For one thing, complications of STDs may be lifelong, and they often emerge years after initial infection. Pelvic inflammatory disease, for instance, starts as an infection of the cervix, then moves into the upper genital tract and fallopian tubes. Eventually it leads to chronic pelvic pain, life-threatening ectopic pregnancy or infertility.

What's more, the demographics are shifting. With large numbers of people divorcing and re-entering the dating scene, "The risk of infection among older folks is higher than most people want to admit," according to Linda Alexander, president and CEO of the American Social Health Association. ASHA's hotlines get calls from 40-year-olds getting herpes and 30-year-olds becoming infected with HIV, she said.

Panelists pointed out, too, that many older employees have dependents who are at risk. An employer campaign that focuses on education, prevention, screening and early treatment can help protect workers' children as well.

## Spreading the Word

Employers can play a key role in removing the stigma that has kept sexually transmitted diseases from being adequately addressed. Begin by talking openly, as you would about any other health care issue, recommends Roger Merrill. "It's too important to allow ourselves to be sidetracked by notions of what 'nice' people do."

At the same time, it's crucial to recognize and respect employees' need for confidentiality in discussing this sensitive subject. Posting or disseminating the numbers of STD hotlines is a good place to start. Distributing literature such as a disease identification list also can help de-stigmatize STDs and open a dialogue.

Informing employees that the National Committee for Quality Assurance added chlamydia screening to its list of Health Plan Employer Data and Information Set (HEDIS) measures in 2000 is another way to broach the subject. You might point out—to upper management and workers alike—that the committee's decision to add this measure attests to the importance of early detection and treatment of a disease that women might otherwise remain unaware of for years.

In making a plea for plain talk, Alexander lamented "the politics of STDs." To get program funding, she said, "We've had to phrase conditions in politically palatable terms." Thus, chlamydia screening is coined infertility prevention. A Pap smear is called a test for cervical cancer, and few women realize they're actually tested for HPV.

The same is true for the Hepatitis B vaccine. "Two thirds of new cases are transmitted sexually," Alexander noted. "But we don't want to tell parents that Hepatitis B is an STD, so we talk to them about liver cancer instead."

On the other hand, dropping euphemistic language is long overdue. "Open discussion of, and access to, information regarding sexual behaviors, their health consequences and methods for protecting against STDs must occur" for sexual norms to change, the Institute of Medicine declared in a 1997 report titled "The Hidden Epidemic: Confronting Sexually Transmitted Diseases."

HEDIS 2000 revealed that less than one in five women eligible for chlamydia screening—all those between ages 15 to 25 who are sexually active—actually receive the test. The numbers reveal the need to put more pressure on health plans and health care providers to promote testing. Talk alone is not enough. . . .

## A Few Corporate Strategies

To get the most bang for the buck, savvy employers have found, contracting and communication should go hand in hand. Perdue Farms, which Merrill describes as "an activist employer," does both. "Our product is health—not just medical care," he told attendees.

New employees discover that on their first day on the job, when an occupational health nurse talks to them about everything from back pain to exercise, environment, seat belts and sexually transmitted disease. "Being uncomfortable with the topic is not a reason to fail to address it," Merrill added.

Perdue follows up with ongoing wellness programs, often selecting a disease of the month. "When it's diabetes, we'll stick your finger. When it's STDs, we set up tables and talk to employees in much the same way. It's important to use the same format to avoid stigmatization," Merrill explains.

Perdue uses various ploys to attract people to programs dealing with this sensitive subject. "We talk about the prevalence and the risk in terms of, 'your kids, your kids' friends,'" Merrill acknowledged. "We don't say, 'Do you have a sexually transmitted disease?'"

Perdue also has a wellness center—actually, a full-service medical facility, where employees and dependents can get care for a copay.

Many women have their annual Pap smears done at the center and can get screening for other STDs as well. The medical records are kept strictly confidential, Merrill emphasized, but employees with privacy concerns can seek care in another setting—for which the company will cover the cost.

IBM also talks to its employees about STDs, often online, said Dottie Robinson, a nurse working in the firm's global occupational health services. "Our Intranet is a powerful communication tool," noted

Robinson, who is responsible for building the corporate giant's web health page. "We get over 15,000 hits a week."

From the first page developed, she added, "We recognized the need to include information about sexually transmitted diseases." STDs have had a spot on the site, called Global Medic, from its inception.

"The page highlights nine sexually transmitted diseases and provides links to experts like the National Institutes of Health, the Centers for Disease Control and Prevention and the American Social Health Association," she said.

Global Medic also features an interactive tool with symptom analysis. "If you're concerned about a symptom, you can describe it and get a response telling you it's urgent or it can wait."

Sexually transmitted disease is one of a number of "personal well-being" topics occasionally highlighted on the web site and promoted to employees via e-mail communications or newsletters. "Ergonomics got the highest response," Robinson recalled. "STDs got one of the lowest."

But that doesn't mean the campaign was unsuccessful, she's quick to point out. "We know that half of those who looked at the STD material went on to seek more information."

IBM's attempts to address STDs extend to its facilities around the globe. In South Africa, the firm is launching a huge AIDS campaign, Robinson reported. Employees in Europe receive brochures and other materials about sexually transmitted diseases.

# Stress Reduction May Control the Recurrence of Genital Herpes

Martin Kohl

A study published in 1999 reveals that persistent stress increases the recurrence of genital herpes, reports Martin Kohl in the following selection. Researchers still do not know the exact mechanism of genital herpes recurrences, but they do know that the virus must be triggered out of its latent state, and long-term stress appears to do so. The author of the study, Kohl writes, encourages physicians to refer their patients with genital herpes to programs that help them learn how to manage their stress. Kohl is a staff columnist for *Dermatology Times*.

Reducing long-term stress through counseling or other stress reduction techniques can stop the recurrence of genital herpes, according to a study by Frances Cohen, Ph.D. and colleagues.

## Measuring the Effects of Long-Term Stress

Dr. Cohen's study, published in Vol. 159 (1999) of the *Archives of Internal Medicine*, indicated that in 58 women, aged 20 to 44: "Persistent stressors and highest level of anxiety predicted genital herpes recurrence, whereas transient mood state, short-term stressors and life change events did not. Women with herpes can be reassured that short-term stressful life experiences and dysphoric mood states do not put them at risk for increased outbreaks of recurrent genital herpes."

The study, Dr. Cohen explained, defined long-term stress as stressful events lasting more than seven days.

"We wanted people to identify situations that they thought were stressful. We asked them to write down descriptions of situations that had occurred in their life that they found to be either stressful, difficult, or problematic for them," said Dr. Cohen, health psychology program, department of psychiatry, University of California at San Francisco School of Medicine.

"Stress, in our study, is self-defined and had to be something the person could describe. Our definition of stress, therefore, was quite different than a response-based definition that labels a person "stressed" based on the person having a high level of adrenocortical hormones, for example," she said.

## Encouraging Stress Reduction

Since the research found that persistent, but not short-term stressors, increased the risk of recurrence of genital herpes lesions, Dr. Cohen suggested that dermatologists ask patients if they are experiencing ongoing, persistent stressors in their lives or frequently experiencing high levels of anxiety. If the answer is yes, the physician could refer the patient to counseling or provide a list of community resources offering help with life problems.

Dr. Cohen said that "counseling or stress reduction activities may be beneficial to patients. Patients can be encouraged to try to do something actively to bring about a solution to an ongoing problem or to look at it in a different way. Also useful would be stress reduction programs including those that focus on exercise and relaxation. These may help to reduce some of the physiological consequences of long-term stressors."

The antiviral drug, acyclovir, can be taken prophylactically to prevent recurrences, but many patients are reluctant to take such drugs long-term. "However, for patients undergoing chronic stress that cannot be resolved through counseling, it might be beneficial to suggest medications like acyclovir to suppress the recurrences," Dr. Cohen added.

It is still unknown exactly what physiological mechanisms are involved in herpes recurrences, although it's been hypothesized that lesions are the result of a two-stage process, she noted.

Dr. Cohen said: "First, the latent virus must be activated, that is, be triggered out of latency. Stress may be involved in that central process. The virus then travels down the ganglion to the site where it has occurred previously. Activated viruses could be blocked by immunological defenses at the local site, and the recrudescence [a new outbreak] would not occur. Thus, the second phase of the hypothesis suggests that if at the local level the immunological controls fail, recurrence would follow. Stress could also be implicated here, since psychoneuroimmunology, [the study of the interaction between behavioral and neural factors and the immune system], studies have shown that chronic stressors affect parameters of the immune system.

Dr. Cohen's study also found that short-term stressful life experiences and negative moods did not increase the likelihood of genital herpes recurrences in women.

# CORNERING A KILLER

Jonathan Fahey

The human papillomavirus (HPV) is responsible for cervical cancers that kill five thousand women in the United States each
year, writes Jonathan Fahey in the following selection. HPV
shows no symptoms while it slowly multiplies within the cells of
the genital tract, and the immune system does not see the cells
as a threat, says Fahey. However, scientists are working on a vaccine to prevent HPV despite several obstacles. Because the virus
can not be grown in tissue cultures like other viruses, says Fahey,
researchers have had to coax organisms into producing a protein
that mimics HPV so that the immune system will attack it. Fahey
is a senior reporter for *Forbes*, a business news magazine.

Chemotherapy, radiation, surgery—oncologists try everything to treat
cervical cancer. Yet of 470,000 women who contract the disease
worldwide each year (15,000 in the U.S.), half die within five years.
This cancer kills 200,000 women annually (5,000 in the U.S.); it's one
of the biggest cancer killers of women in the world.

Yet virtually all the cases are avoidable, even preventable: The cancer is caused by a sexually transmitted disease (STD) known as HPV
(human papillomavirus). Insidious and prodigious, HPV is the fastest-
spreading STD. More than half of all sexually active Americans will
carry the virus at some point in their lives. Every year up to 40 million
people get infected with 1 of 20 sibling strains.

## A Stealthy Virus

Condoms don't do much to stop HPV because the virus can easily
spread through incidental skin contact. No reliable tests exist. And
there is no treatment or cure; scientists aren't even sure whether, once
HPV infects a person, it dies away entirely or merely lies dormant. Usually the virus runs its course in a year or so without severe symptoms—
men, in particular, rarely realizing that they've got it, blithely pass it on
to their partners. "It is a very clever virus," says Kathrin Jansen, a scien-
tist at Merck. "Your immune system doesn't even see it. People don't
know if they're infected. That makes it even easier to spread around."

Researchers first discovered more than a decade ago that HPV causes cancers of the cervix, anus and genitalia. But government and corporate labs didn't exactly wage war on the rapidly spreading agent. "It's like a stepchild compared with other viruses," Jansen says. "It hardly gets any attention."

But at long last scientists are close to creating vaccines that could stop HPV cold, with the potential to eliminate 75% of cervical cancer cases. At Merck, where Jansen runs the program to create an HPV vaccine, scientists are expected to begin final-phase human trials of one promising candidate. GlaxoSmithKline is also expected soon to put its vaccine into final trials.

"The vaccines are very well developed, and the prospects of success in the near future are very exciting," says J. Thomas Cox, executive medical director of the National HPV & Cervical Cancer Resource Center in Research Triangle Park, North Carolina.

The vaccines target the two HPV strains that are responsible for 75% of cervical cancers. Merck's also targets two other strains that cause nearly all forms of genital warts. The potential market is huge: Some 1.4 million cases of genital warts are reported each year in the U.S., and HPV infection is present in 10% to 15% of women aged 16 to 25.

HPV is a stealth operator. It enters the body through tiny breaks in the skin caused by rubbing during sex, making its way below the surface to worm inside immature skin cells in and around the genital tract. HPV bides its time, slowly multiplying inside these cells as they mature, transforming them into insidious envelopes stuffed with millions of copies of the invader. Once these carrier skin cells mature and die, the body's immune system, failing to notice the HPV hordes inside, no longer perceives them as a threat. That is when the virus releases its attack, spreading when the dead skin cells flake off the body naturally.

Some strains cause lesions on the cervix, and, for reasons that mystify researchers, some of the lesions turn cancerous. Solving that puzzle could yield treatments, but perfecting a potent vaccine would be a preemptive—and far more effective—form of attack.

HPV is so widespread in the U.S. that cervical cancer might have soared far beyond current levels were it not for the Pap smear. This test lets doctors catch cervical lesions early and snip them away before they can become malignant. But the tests are infrequently administered in the developing world, and even in the U.S. they are notoriously inaccurate, failing to spot infected cervical cells 25% of the time. Pap tests and other forms of HPV management are also expensive, costing Americans at least $6 billion a year. A positive result often leads to the removal of large sections of the cervix, either as a precaution or after cancer is found.

Because of the virus' quirks, a vaccine for HPV long seemed impossible. Vaccines are usually some form of a weakened or dead virus grown from living tissue cultures and injected into the bloodstream. Much like giving a bloodhound a sample sniff of an outlaw's clothes, vaccines teach the immune system what to attack when a real infection comes. But HPV is a different bug altogether: It is the only known virus that can't be grown in tissue cultures. Because it develops only in cells that are maturing, it can be grown only in living mammals.

## Coaxing Cells to Resemble a Killer

Breakthroughs came in the early 1990s, when researchers at several academic labs succeeded in teaching organisms, such as silkworms, to produce proteins that look exactly like strains of HPV. This discovery inspired HPV vaccine programs at such drug giants as Merck and small biotechs as MedImmune in Gaithersburg, Maryland, which supplies the GlaxoSmithKline vaccine.

At Merck, Kathrin Jansen started the HPV vaccine program and has shepherded it through eight years of development. In 1993 she and her colleagues began inserting genes into yeast cells to coax them into producing proteins that form the exterior coat of the nastier HPV strains. The proteins naturally twist themselves into particles that are indistinguishable from HPV. When these harmless particles are injected into the bloodstream, the immune system starts pumping out antibodies trained to eliminate HPV.

Early on Merck ambitiously pursued an antiviral cocktail containing four vaccines: two against cancer, two against genital warts. The vaccine has been powerful in human tests, stimulating up to 150 times the body's normal immune response to HPV. Two and a half years after Merck gave its vaccine to several hundred 16- to 23-year-old women in a recent trial, none had become infected with the strain they had been vaccinated against; 5% had become infected with another common cancerous strain. A small test, but it has sparked larger trials.

Researchers caution that the vaccines [may not be available until 2006]—if they work at all. Vaccines are notoriously difficult to test: Instead of simply measuring signs of healing, testers must prove a negative: that someone won't get a disease. That will take rigorous testing of several thousand women over the next few years. With HPV it is even more difficult, because cervical cancer takes years to develop.

Darron Brown, who is testing the Merck vaccine at Indiana University, worries that the cells in the cervix are too far from the blood supply to be surrounded by enough antibodies to fight off the virus. Jansen counters that the abrasions that open the door to HPV also attract enough blood to carry in the army of antibodies.

Even if they are effective, vaccines may face stiff resistance from parents who are urged to let their 11-year-old daughter get a shot against a sexually transmitted disease or told that their son needs one for a disease that is likely never to harm him. But the payoff could be lucrative for Merck or whichever drugmaker leads the way. For millions of girls who are now just toddlers, the benefits will make the researchers' struggle all the more worthwhile.

# CHAPTER 4

# FACING THE CHALLENGES OF SEXUALLY TRANSMITTED DISEASES: PERSONAL STORIES

Contemporary Issues
Companion

# Uncovering the Silent Suffering of a Teen with Chlamydia

Sheri Fink

Sheri Fink is a doctor of emergency medicine and has been involved in emergency assistance programs in Bosnia, Chechnya, and Mozambique. In the following selection, Fink describes the challenge of diagnosing the symptoms of the sexually transmitted disease (STD), chlamydia, which has brought her teenaged patient to the emergency room. Because the symptoms of the disease are often mild, she writes, treatment can be delayed, increasing the patient's chance of developing pelvic inflammatory disease (PID). According to Fink, her patient was experiencing the chronic pain that accompanies PID. Although the young girl had recently been treated for a chlamydial infection, her doctors maintained her right to keep her sexual activity private, and the girl's parents seemed unaware of the problem, Fink reveals. The risk of infection could be reduced if teens felt safe to discuss their sexuality, says Fink, but many parents fail to talk with teens about STDs.

"Here we go again," Ron Smith said with a sigh. "This is the third time we've been to the emergency room in five weeks."

He nodded toward his 15-year-old daughter. "Lorna's got a stomachache. She's throwing up. The last time she came here, it was a problem with her appendix."

Lorna lay on the stretcher, looking away from her father. She slid me a blasé look.

## Examining the Clues

"The pain you're having now," I asked, "when did it start?"

"Two days ago. I thought it was from something I ate at a diner."

"Did your friends get sick?"

She shook her head. "No."

"How is the pain this time compared to the other times you were here?"

"Not as bad," she said.

The nurse's chart said Lorna's vital signs were normal and she had no fever. I placed my hands on her abdomen and began to press.

"Tell me where it's sore."

No response. Her belly felt soft against my fingertips, not hard as it does when a patient guards against pain or when an infection irritates abdominal muscles.

A complete exam yielded only two subtle abnormalities. When I listened with my stethoscope, the clicks and gurgles of her bowel sounds were less frequent than normal. Tapping the right lower side of her belly with my fingertips produced a dull sound. The sign meant something solid beneath the tissue, anything from feces to a mass.

And I noticed something else. Lorna and her father did not speak or even look at each other, and I wondered if this could offer us a clue.

In the ER, woman plus abdominal pain equals pregnancy outside the uterus until proven otherwise. Known as an ectopic pregnancy, it occurs when a fetus implants in the wrong place, often causing massive internal bleeding. An emergency physician's biggest responsibility is to rule out just such urgent, dangerous conditions.

I looked at Lorna, who seemed young, innocent, and irked. Awkwardness nearly prevented me from asking my next questions. "Is there any chance you could be pregnant?"

"No," she said.

Abdominal pain is one of medicine's most formidable diagnostic challenges. Most abdominal disorders lack specific symptoms and signs, and even advanced imaging techniques cannot always portray a condition as common as appendicitis. Answers often do not come until a patient undergoes surgery.

I called up Lorna's medical records on the hospital computer. Just as her father said, Lorna had visited the hospital twice over the past month for abdominal pain due to a suspected ruptured appendix. The report also indicated that although the suspected rupture had created a pocket of infection, the illness appeared to be subsiding. So the surgeons made the rare choice not to operate; instead they gave Lorna a strong mixture of antibiotics. They planned to remove the diseased appendix several weeks later.

## Uncovering the Damage

But Lorna's father had failed to mention that fluid collected from a pelvic exam during Lorna's first hospitalization had tested positive for the parasite chlamydia. That meant she was probably sexually active, because the parasite is almost always transmitted via sexual intercourse.

Doctors had treated Lorna with the antibiotic azithromycin to kill the chlamydia, but gynecologists suspected that the infection, rather than a ruptured appendix, might have caused Lorna's abdominal pain and hospital admissions.

The attending physician and I returned to perform a pelvic examination. Lorna had no masses and no pain when I manipulated her uterus and felt for her ovaries. I asked if she wanted to tell us anything without her father present.

"No."

Outside the room, the attending physician asked me what I thought. Lorna no longer had abdominal pain, she did not have a fever, and she was already on antibiotics. The possibility of a recurrent bacterial infection was unlikely. Given her sexual activity, we needed to rule out an ectopic pregnancy—unlikely too. I began to think Lorna might have been right about the bad meal.

Had the lab tests come out negative and Lorna kept down some food, we might very well have sent her home. But the attending suggested I notify the surgeons who took care of Lorna last time.

"I can't get down to see her for another half hour," said the surgical resident. "Can you get started on X rays?"

I ordered them and went to lunch. When I returned, I found the surgeon preparing to admit Lorna. He asked for a CT scan, a radiological study that provides slicelike internal images of the body by gathering X-ray transmission data from many different directions.

The X-rays showed a blockage in Lorna's small bowel. The surgeon planned to run a tube from Lorna's nose into her stomach to decompress the built-up fluid and gas. Her bowel function, he said, should return to normal in a few days, and she could go home.

The next morning I learned that Lorna had not gone up to the patient floor. The results of the CT scan had sent her right into the operating room.

Despite the lack of a palpable mass on her slender frame, the CT revealed a huge abscess in the right side of her pelvis. Her immune system had corralled microbes into a circumscribed area, so she failed to show signs of infection such as fever, faster heart rate, and intense pain. But the infected fluid had pressed on her bowels, causing tissues to stick together and obstruct fecal movement.

An abscess usually develops next to a diseased organ. When the surgeons drained the fluid and freed the adhering tissues, they found Lorna's abscess had originated not from her appendix but from the fallopian tube near her right ovary. The antibiotic had failed to cure Lorna's infection because it was so advanced. The cause of Lorna's medical troubles was now clear: chlamydia.

Chlamydia is the most commonly reported sexually transmitted disease in the United States, with an estimated 4 million new cases each year. Certain subtypes of the parasite *Chlamydia trachomatis* infect the epithelial cells lining the reproductive tract. The organisms grow inside the cells, killing them, and the body's immune response leads to inflammation and further local damage.

## Suffering in Silence

Chlamydia causes such mild initial symptoms that doctors detect most infections late or incidentally on routine testing. Delays in diagnosis and treatment increase the chance that the pathogen will spread up the reproductive organs to infect the cells that line the tubes and ovaries, causing pelvic inflammatory disease. About 20 percent of such patients end up with chronic pelvic pain. A similar number develop scarring in the fallopian tubes, which prevents conception. Lorna faced some tough possibilities.

I stopped in to see Lorna later that day. She talked a little, but clammed up when her parents appeared. When I left the room, the Smiths followed me.

"What caused this?" asked Mrs. Smith.

Despite Lorna's three hospital admissions, her parents had barely an inkling of their daughter's sexually transmitted infection. Doctors had respected Lorna's legal right to keep medical information about her sexual activity private. I urged her mother to speak with Lorna.

"I try, but I can't. When it was time to give her the menstruation talk a few years ago, she said 'I know it all' and ran out of the room. I was so relieved!"

Parents and physicians often fail to talk with teens about sexual activity and sexual disease transmission. Condoms reduce the risk of infection. Douching after sex increases it. And vaccinations against hepatitis B, which is sexually transmitted, are available.

"It's so hard to know what they're doing," Lorna's father said. "You can't keep them locked up, and we have to work." He looked down the hall. "Anyhow, I hope this will take care of it."

# A Young Woman Learns to Live with Genital Herpes

Holly Becker

Holly Becker is a national correspondent for *SEX, ETC.*, an online sexuality and health newsletter written by teens for teens. In the following selection, Becker tells the story of how she contracted genital herpes and learned to live with the sexually transmitted disease. Becker recounts the emotional and physical pain she experienced when she was diagnosed with genital herpes. Because her genital area was inflamed and swollen, Becker explains, she experienced excruciating pain when the doctor took swabs to make a diagnosis. Moreover, some people thought that because she had genital herpes, she was promiscuous. Many do not understand, says Becker, that anyone can get the disease, not just those who have many sexual partners. Although the disease can be managed, there is no cure, Becker reports, but she hopes sharing her experience will help others better understand the disease.

"It will never happen to me."

I used to tell myself this about sexually transmitted diseases—before I contracted the herpes virus. But first, let me start with a little story.

## From Trust to Fear

His name was Derek [whose name has been changed], and I knew him from work. He was 22 and I was 17. Tall and skinny, he wasn't the cutest guy, but his character made him attractive. He was funny, very charismatic, and he treated me well. He made me feel like I was someone to be noticed. To guys at work, he would say, "Wow, boys, look at that girl. Isn't she somethin'?" He gave me special attention to boost my self-esteem. He would say things like, "You're so beautiful." Whenever another girl was around, he'd ignore them and only pay attention to me. Derek was my friend, and I trusted him.

About a month after we started hanging out, we had sex for the first time. I asked him that question: "Have you been tested?" He swore to me that he had. "I'm clean," he said. He didn't get specific about when he was last tested. I still asked him to wear a condom.

A little while into the sex, I could tell he hadn't put on a condom. I knew then that I'd made a mistake, but I didn't stop him. I was embarrassed and afraid of being rejected. I thought about treatable diseases, like chlamydia, and figured that if Derek had anything, then I'd already gotten it and the damage was done.

## A Painful Discovery

I started noticing some differences with my body. Pains and smells that hadn't been there before. Derek and I still slept together without a condom. I kept thinking that the damage was already done. And I wasn't serious with him; we were very casual. So I didn't say anything. I figured there was no way I could get anything serious, like herpes, HIV, or syphilis. I was also nervous. I'd never been to a gynecologist, just to my doctor for checkups, and I was too afraid to tell my mother what I was doing.

The symptoms were unbearable and the pain got worse. I couldn't urinate without screaming out loud. My abdominal pain brought tears to my eyes. While working alone one day, I got very sick. I called my mother and asked her to come get me. I finally told her about my symptoms. We went to a gynecologist first thing the next morning.

Thank God for my supportive mother. She held my hand while I screamed in pain as the doctor took a Pap smear and culture. It felt like torture. Imagine this: your entire insides are swollen and inflamed, and someone puts just a slight amount of pressure on that swelling and inflammation. It feels like someone just rammed a sword into you. I have never felt anything so horrible.

After seeing the open lesions that were down there, the doctor said that there was a good chance it was genital herpes. He was certain that I had a raging case of Pelvic Inflammatory Disease (PID), which is sometimes caused by an STD.

"Genital herpes?" I thought. "He must be wrong; he's just trying to scare me. Am I the type of girl who gets herpes? Who is?"

## Learning About Herpes

Herpes is a sexually transmitted disease that's caused by the herpes simplex virus (HSV). HSV-type 1, or oral herpes, normally causes fever blisters on the mouth or face. HSV-type 2, or genital herpes, usually affects the vagina, penis, and/or anus. Herpes viruses are usually "inactive" and cause no symptoms. But sometimes, the viruses cause "outbreaks" of fluid-filled blisters and lesions.

Once a person is infected with herpes, he or she has it for life.

Genital herpes is *not* uncommon. If you look at the percentage of adolescents and adults who have it, you might even consider it normal. Across the United States, 45 million sexually active people ages 12 and older—that's one out of five of the total adolescent and adult population—are infected with HSV-2. And genital herpes is more common in sexually active females—approximately one out of four of us are infected with it.

But even though herpes is so widespread, the general feeling in society is that there's something really wrong with you if you become infected. Like you had to sleep with at least five people, instead of just the one person who gave it to you. The common perception is that you're obviously a "slut" if you get genital herpes. But I slept with one person and I got it.

Most people don't know that you can live with and manage herpes. Every once in a while, especially when you're stressed, you'll get outbreaks of tiny lesions or blisters on your genitals. If you have sex during this time, you're likely to transmit the virus to your partner. You can also transmit herpes to a sexual partner *before* and *after* you break out in sores, until the sores have healed. But you can't get herpes from a toilet seat, a towel, or clothing. These are myths.

If you're going to have oral sex or intercourse, *always* use a latex condom or dental dam the correct way. But remember, condoms don't completely protect you from herpes. If a guy has genital herpes, for instance, the condom won't cover lesions that appear on his scrotum or testicles. So abstaining from sex is sometimes the best thing to do.

## Live and Learn

I ended up confronting Derek. I felt he needed to know what he had done, so he would use a condom from then on. We dated for a little while longer. Then he decided to go back to his ex-girlfriend. We're no longer friends.

Each day, I try to deal with the fact that I have herpes. And when people put me down or treat me like I'm different, it makes coping with it even harder. Herpes has especially changed my life when it comes to relationships. You never know when you're supposed to tell someone and if they will freak out.

After I was diagnosed, I started dating an old boyfriend again. When I told him about it, he acted like he was fine with it. But the next day, he started being really distant. Then I found out he told a lot of people, which really hurt. Whenever someone acted weird toward me, I wondered if it was because they knew.

One time, my old boyfriend's friend was in class with me and started talking really loudly about me to another person in the room. "Yeah, she's a whore and has herpes from some guy she knew for like an hour," he said. "Guess that taught her to keep her legs shut." I had to leave the room I was crying so hard.

When I first got the virus, I thought, "Who would want to ever marry a girl with herpes?"

But the more I am open with people about it, the more I learn that it's OK. I know that someone will love me for me and not care that I have herpes, because the virus doesn't make me who I am. Still, sometimes I avoid relationships altogether, for fear of rejection. And that makes me lonely.

So, think about my story when you're having sex. Ask your future partners the hard questions, too. Ask them about their sexual past, when they were tested, for what, and, since then, what they've done to protect themselves.

And think about my story when you hear that someone has an STD. Most likely, if they have one, they are scared and lonely, and could use a friend.

# Six Dancers Living with AIDS

Wendy Perron

During the early years of the AIDS epidemic, the dance community lost many prominent artists to AIDS, writes Wendy Perron, who is herself a dancer, a choreographer, and editor of *Dance Magazine*. However, Perron explains, medical advances have given those diagnosed with AIDS the opportunity to live longer, more productive lives. In the following selection, Perron recounts the experiences of six dancers who are living with AIDS. Some remain optimistic, she says, and have used the experience as motivation to accelerate their careers; others are torn between the threat of death and the often debilitating side effects of medication. Whatever choices each makes, says Perron, most focus on improving the quality of their lives. One of the greatest fears these dancers face is people's reactions when and if they disclose their diagnosis; sometimes, Perron reports, those outside the dance community shun them, but as a rule, people respond favorably, and many of these dancers enjoy being available to answer questions and help educate the public on HIV and AIDS.

I was riding in an elevator in a Manhattan hospital, and the elevator doors happened to open onto a ward in which a distraught young man was talking into the phone at the nurses' station. I recognized him as a fellow choreographer—Arnie Zane. I knew Arnie had AIDS, and I stepped out to say hello. He had just learned that his chemotherapy wasn't working and the doctors were telling him there wasn't much hope. He was crying, and I hugged him. That was all I could do. As we walked outside, he lamented, "I know I complain a lot, but I love this life and I don't want to die." A few months later, Arnie was dead.

That was in 1987. If this scene had happened today, there would be more hope.

In the '80s and '90s, the dance community was decimated by AIDS. We lost some of our most treasured elders: Alvin Ailey, Robert Joffrey, Rudolf Nureyev, Michael (*A Chorus Line*) Bennett; some of our most promising youths: Edward Stierle of the Joffrey and Peter Fonseca of American Ballet Theatre, and mid-career artists like Arnie Zane (whose

From "Living with AIDS: Six Dancers Share Their Stories," by Wendy Perron, *Dance Magazine*, December 2000. Copyright © 2000 by *Dance Magazine*. Reprinted with permission.

memory is preserved in the name of the Bill T. Jones/Arnie Zane Dance Company), Louis Falco, Robert Blankshine, Christopher Gillis, John Berndt and Ulysses Dove. During that period, it seems, we were attending as many memorial services as dance performances. We learned the meaning of community—the gathering together when the loss of someone you love leaves a big hole.

But thanks to improved medication, testing positive for HIV is no longer a death sentence. More dancers are continuing to live and dance with the virus. Others are still having a hard time. The fatality rate is slowing, but we cannot forget the devastation the disease still brings. I spoke with six dancers and former dancers who are handling the disease in different ways.

## An Educator's Story

Dancer/choreographer Neil Greenberg, who teaches at the State University of New York [SUNY] at Purchase, tested positive in 1986. He's been basically asymptomatic, so he is living his life as usual, only cutting back on alcohol. Greenberg says 1993 was a hard year for him: His brother died of AIDS, two-thirds of the people in his HIV support group died, and he learned that the virus's presence in his blood had increased. Out of these tragedies emerged his *Not-About-AIDS-Dance* (1994) a powerful work that created a buzz in downtown New York. But in 1997 he landed in the hospital. "I had high fevers the whole week I was performing that fall," he says. "About a year later the doctors realized it was the medication that was doing that to me."

Now on new medication, he is thriving again. All along, he says, he has maintained a positive approach. "I tried to deny what all of the papers said, which was a ten-year maximum life expectancy," Greenberg says. "I refused to believe that and, as it turned out, I was right, for myself." However, he still struggles with the disease emotionally: "The whole AIDS-as-punishment thing is hard to get rid of in the deepest layers, and I probably haven't." In order to dispel some of the stigma that he grew up with, he makes a point of telling his freshman students at SUNY Purchase that he has the virus. After all, he reasons, it's part of their education.

## Living a Normal Life

Another dancer I spoke with dances every night in a high-powered Broadway musical. He has asked that his name be withheld, so I'll call him Jack. Jack got the bad news in 1996, the year that new medications came into being and many AIDS patients found "cocktails" of a variety of medications to be effective, Jack says. "My doctor told me right away, 'This isn't the end of your life. Don't drive your car off a cliff. There are medications that are helping people, and you should be able to live a normal life. It's a controlled disease like diabetes. You just have to take your pills every day.'" At first Jack balked at telling his fellow dancers. But, he said, "I've never had a bad reaction from people I've been working with, though it's scary at first. You're afraid that people will look at you differently. But I don't mind being out a little bit at work, because people have questions and they know they can come to me. I enjoy giving back whatever I can to people around me." He's been generally very healthy, but his doctors haven't always known what to prescribe: "One time, for a whole month, I couldn't leave the couch: vomiting, diarrhea, severe stomach cramps. It was very scary."

But the knowledge of his HIV status motivated him. "It made me pull my life together and get my career going. I was happy doing revues and competitions, but I decided I wanted to make Broadway. Within three months, I made Broadway."

He feels comfortable in the dance world. "Being gay in the dance world is more accepted and you can be who you are. Because of that, people who are [HIV] positive can come out and share that also. When you get into TV or film, being gay is not OK. They may hire you to be a gay character, but they want you to be straight. If they were to find out you're HIV [positive], they would probably not hire you."

## A Firebird's Friends and Foes

Of course, not only gay men get the disease. Stephanie Dabney, former star and unforgettable Firebird with Dance Theatre of Harlem [DTH] in the early 1980s, was diagnosed ten years ago. Her first thoughts were, "There goes my career. If I get too sick to dance, what am I going to do? How am I going to tell my brother and sister?" She spent all of 1996 in the hospital with recurring pneumonia, and the following year in nursing homes. "My fourth pneumonia was PCP [pneumocystis carinii pneumonia, a life-threatening infection for people with weakened immune systems], and my lung collapsed. I had a chest tube pump in me for eight weeks. I remember the doctor coming into my room, surprised, saying 'Hi, I didn't think you would be here.' He thought I wasn't going to make it through the night! That freaked me out." She is now participating in an experimental program, a nine-month trial with an Italian physician. "Maybe I'll help him find the cure," she says. Friends encourage her to resume dancing. "I ran into [actress] Cicely Tyson, and she thinks I should dance again," she says. "But Arthur [Mitchell, DTH's artistic director] has young, healthy and eager dancers now, and there's nowhere else I would want to dance besides DTH. I can't imagine trying to get in shape. I'd rather be remembered as the Firebird when I was young and healthy."

Sometimes, non-dancers would turn against her when they found out she had AIDS. "There was a woman in Atlanta whose position was to wine and dine the Somebodies," Dabney says. "I was the black ballerina who did *Firebird*, so I was in her in-crowd. But when she found out I had it, she wouldn't even return my calls."

Dabney, who has taught at Spelman College in Atlanta, thinks about the future. "I thought I'd want to teach again, but I'm walking with canes now. Tanaquil LeClerq [the extraordinary young Balanchine ballerina who was struck down with polio in the '50s] was my favorite teacher. She used her hands and arms as legs and feet."

## From Near Death to Rebirth

Another former dancer, Joseph Carman, is now a freelance writer. Carman, who has danced with American Ballet Theatre and the Joffrey, almost died four years ago before the new medications became available. He had been diagnosed in 1987 while dancing with the Metropolitan Opera Ballet. "I kept it secret in the beginning because there was such a stigma. That was the time when *The Post* was running headlines like 'AIDS Killer.' There weren't many support groups around. The year before I left the company, I told the ballet mistress, Diana Levy. The Americans with Disabilities Act had just been approved, which protects anyone in the work force who has a disability. It allows people with HIV to shorten work hours or to do a less demanding job. She was understanding and would ask me during rehearsal, 'Are you OK?'" The main thing for Carman was getting enough rest. Working on a new production, he'd sometimes be in the theater for twelve hours: "When things were bad, I'd break out in shingles."

In 1996, he was diagnosed with Kaposi's sarcoma (KS), a cancerous growth associated with AIDS. "It progressed slowly and then all of a sudden my immune system went like a house of cards. I'd wake up with two new lesions every day. It was terrifying. They discovered I had KS in my lungs. That usually means a year to live if you're lucky. The doctor put me in the hospital and administered heavy-duty chemotherapy. I call it 'slash-and-burn' chemo because it wrecks everything. For days afterward I would feel like crawling out of my skin. But it did get rid of the tumors."

An AIDS conference in Geneva had just demonstrated that protease inhibitors and the new "cocktails" were helping people. It was good timing, and Carman started a regime of the new medications. "My immune system slowly started to rebuild itself, and my T-cells [white blood cells that help suppress disease] climbed from 10 to over 600. It's truly miraculous." But it wasn't easy emotionally. "I thought I was dying, and then all of a sudden I wasn't dying. I was in shock for about a year. Physically, it took me four years to feel like myself again."

But Carman has been through a significant shift. "When you come that close to death, it changes the way you look at things. It's like a rebirth: it cuts the b—s—factor. For me now, the quality of life is important: eating well, walking my dog in the park, spending time with my boyfriend. I still do a juggling act with all my medications."

Carman feels that consciousness has been raised and there is less stigma about the disease. He is grateful for the concern of people in the dance world. But the past is a string of sorrows. American Ballet Theatre's 1977 video of *The Nutcracker* starring Mikhail Baryshnikov and Gelsey Kirkland used to be broadcast on TV every Christmas. He says, "I can't even watch it now because half the dancers in it are dead."

## Making Short-Term Plans

Chris Dohse, a dancer/choreographer/writer who is also a proofreader, is torn between submitting to the new medications and just letting himself slide downhill. "I don't know if I want to buckle myself into the regime of the new cocktails. I don't want to go through that ordeal." Dohse, who tested positive in 1987 when he was dancing in Washington, D.C., was put on azidothymidine, or AZT, in 1990. AZT inhibits the multiplication of the AIDS virus, but it can have debilitating side effects. "I felt terrible every single day of that year," Dohse says. "It makes you tired, nauseous, headachy—dizzy and run-down. During that time they were finding that it works better if you take less of it. I got disillusioned and distrustful, so I don't believe anything the doctors say."

But for Dohse too, the news was at first a motivating factor: "Knowing I had the virus made me stop fiddling around. I stopped dancing for other people and started making my own work." Like Greenberg, he used his despair creatively. "I made a big dance for nine people that was going to be the final thing that I gave to the world. I kept revamping it. I didn't want to finish it because then it meant I was going to live, and have to make other work. This was supposed to be the everything-I-have-to-say piece."

He lost the few romantic figures in his life, which has left him with a strong sense of alienation. "Mostly I feel anger that I didn't get to go with them. They had these memorial services and dramatic narrative arcs, but I have to stay here and turn gray and have my teeth fall out and pay back my student loans. I'm lonely." Medically, he's not up for the new round. "They started saying I should take new medication to reduce my viral load. They said that to me in 1990 with the AZT. My blood data will improve but I'll feel awful." His T-cells are under 100, and, after thirteen years, his viral load has gone sky high. Looking back, he says, "Back at eight years the data showed that thirteen years was the longest anybody had lasted before they started getting sick. I thought: OK, I got five years left: I'll make a five-year plan. For eight years I made six-month plans. I would have gotten a college degree back then if I wasn't going to die any day. I danced instead, thinking I'd go out in a blaze of glory. Little did I know I would keep lingering. I'm the boy who cried wolf because I've lived so long on this edge of despair."

## A Matter of Self-Preservation

Christopher Pilafian, on the faculty of the University of California at Santa Barbara, has found some measure of peace. He danced with Jennifer Muller/The Works from its inception in 1974 to 1989, eventually serving as associate artistic director. Now 47, he says, "It's hard to tell whether what I'm feeling is a result of the virus or of the natural aging process. I'm a little more methodical, less rambunctious now." Four years ago, he improved his T-cell count tremendously with the new medications.

Pilafian feels fortunate to have colleagues who are sensitive to his condition. "Once it was made known, the other teachers were totally supportive. When I was having a bad time, they were available to cover classes for me." He regrets the toll the virus has taken on the lives of dancers he admired as well as his own. "The middle years are an important period in a dancer's life: You've still got your chops and also your independence. I would like to have seen what Louis Falco would have done, had he lived past 50. If I weren't HIV positive, I might have focused on my work as a choreographer. Instead, I had to go into self-preservation."

In 1989, he attended a seminar that redefined AIDS not as a terminal illness, but as a manageable chronic infection. "To take the assumption of fatality off the diagnosis is very powerful. Now I'm doing things that support life: meditation, visualization, eating well and watching the purity of things. There was so much fear about the available medicines at that time. To deal with that, I used what I knew from dancing: imagery. I began to visualize the medications as rainbows, waterfalls and light."

"At the conference, we were asked, 'What is this apparent misfortune bringing to you that is a benefit?' It gave permission to look at your life in a different way. You could imagine the endpoint being closer. Then starts the dropping away of the nonessentials, which is a sacred, life-sustaining process."

These six dancers are, like the rest of us, many-faceted people. One of those facets, surely, is tremendous courage. Another is hard-earned wisdom. All of them agree on one thing: the need to tell young people to take precautions. Anyone can contract the virus from sexual activity, and drug users can get it from using a contaminated needle. Although a broad range of treatments is now available, not every patient does well on them, and the side effects can be devastating. The ultimate message is one of prevention: inform yourself, protect yourself, and have only safe sex.

# WOMEN HELPING OTHERS COPE WITH INCURABLE STDS

Leilani Lafaurie

In the following selection, Leilani Lafaurie discusses the experiences of four women who, by creating a forum in which people can share their experiences, help others cope with incurable sexually transmitted diseases (STDs). Two of the women Lafaurie talks with have genital herpes, another was diagnosed with AIDS, and another maintains a relationship with a boyfriend who has genital herpes. Lafaurie reveals how these women contracted or encountered STDs and explores the programs that they support. According to Lafaurie, by sharing their own experiences these women not only help those diagnosed with incurable STDs, particularly women, learn to live with their diseases but help others learn the facts. Lafaurie is a section editor for *FEM*, a feminist magazine published at the University of California, Los Angeles.

Marisa Pollack walked into a bar one night with a group of middle-aged singles. She walked out later that night with a slightly younger man. Then she saved his life.

Marisa works for GotHerpes.com, a Web site dedicated to helping people with herpes break their silence. That night she had organized a social event at the bar for people with herpes, and she met a young man playing pool. He kept asking her questions about her group, sensing that her story about attending a birthday party was somehow awry.

On the ride home, she told him the truth about her work with GotHerpes.com, and he broke down in tears. As it turned out, he also has herpes. He had purchased a gun and was considering suicide to release himself from the disgust and shame he felt because of his disease. Marisa stayed with him, counseling him until six o'clock that morning.

Marisa is one of a handful of women dedicated to breaking down the walls of silence surrounding diseases like herpes and HPV (human papilloma virus). The American Social Health Association (ASHA) states that one in five people in the U.S. has a sexually transmitted disease (STD), and the number continues to climb. The need for a safe space and a dialogue about STDs is apparent, and women like Marisa become increasingly important.

Tammy Morgan, a 20 year-old college student at Mount San Antonio College in Walnut, California is working to break through the silence surrounding herpes. 37 year-old Cathy Olufs is a project coordinator for Women Alive, a peer based counseling group for HIV-positive women. Jennifer [whose name has been changed to protect her privacy], a third-year English major at UCLA, is dating someone who has herpes.

These are extraordinary women accomplishing extraordinary things: they are helping others to lead fulfilling lives with incurable STDs, while finding personal healing and support in the process.

## Hiding Her Secret

Marisa was infected with herpes and HPV by an abusive ex-boyfriend when she was 20 years old. After he sexually assaulted her, he told her that she would never have another boyfriend. When she went to the doctor's office, she found out why.

All she heard the doctor say was that she had contracted two incurable diseases; the rest of the doctor's speech was muffled by her thoughts of imminent death. Because of her experience, Marisa firmly believes therapists, not doctors, should deliver news about STD infection to patients, as well as scheduling mandatory follow-up sessions.

Marisa dropped out of beauty school and joined the circus, traveling across the country "with a bunch of carnies." Marisa, a self-proclaimed small town girl, was able to reinvent herself in the circus. She invented new identities for herself, carefully hiding her secret while pushing men away; she preferred that people think she was gay rather than letting them know her secret.

Marisa felt like she was dying inside and could not stand the thought of dating anyone and passing on her virus. She wanted to die, but she would not commit suicide because "I didn't want my parents to hate me for killing myself." Marisa hid her secret for fourteen and a half years until she found the Antopia Network, the company that created GotHerpes.com.

## Learning to Connect

Tammy, Marisa's employee at GotHerpes.com, exemplifies what Marisa wishes she could have been like at 20 years old. Tammy wants to help people her age create a dialogue about their STDs. "College students are in denial; they aren't talking about it," she says.

Marisa says Tammy is in a much different place than Marisa was at 20, and she attributes that to the Internet. Tammy does not have to hide her secret in shame because she has found a support group. Marisa, now 37, says that it is a different world today than when she was first diagnosed with herpes. "It's not the virus that will kill you,"

Marisa says, "It's keeping that dirty little secret." Today, she and Tammy have the capability to connect with a huge community of people who are living with their virus.

Tammy contracted herpes from her second boyfriend, a "nice guy" and someone she trusted. She says she asked him if he was "clean," not knowing exactly what that meant. Tammy accepts responsibility for her actions saying, "I had sex and I got bit." When she found out about her diagnosis over the phone, she "cried hysterically" and thought about killing herself. "I felt alone," Tammy said, and she embarked on a cross-country journey in her Volkswagen van for seven months.

Tammy says a herpes diagnosis can be emotionally draining, and she "needed that period of time to deal with what happened." By putting things in perspective, Tammy now realizes that she is not a bad person for having contracted the disease; she was just uneducated.

## The Importance of Reaching Out

Unfortunately, the circumstances of Tammy's infection are not uncommon. Cathy contracted HIV from her boyfriend while in a 3-year monogamous relationship.

"This was during the era when everyone still thought it was a gay disease or a junkie disease, and the guy I was with wasn't gay and he didn't use drugs, so I didn't really think that I was at risk. I never insisted on a condom," Cathy said.

Cathy found out that she was HIV positive in 1995 after her relationship had ended. When she delivered the news over the phone, her boyfriend told her that he had known all along, but had been afraid to tell her for fear of losing her. "I have never felt so betrayed," she said.

At the time of Cathy's diagnosis, she didn't know much about HIV and AIDS. She said, "I just thought I was going to die." Today, through her work with Women Alive, she focuses on educating herself about the latest treatments and advancements regarding HIV.

She feels her work as a project coordinator has helped her immensely. "It helped me cope with my own issues by helping other women, and [in that way] we all kind of help each other." She also acknowledges that people who know they have the virus, and were probably infected in college, are not reaching out to educate college students. That makes it easy for college students to distance themselves from the virus even though "there are people walking among them who are living with HIV" and other STDs.

## A Risky Relationship

Jennifer, a UCLA student, met her boyfriend at a party. He told her he had herpes soon into the relationship, before they had sex. She chose not to walk away. They have been together for a little less than a year, and she feels that uninfected people should realize that it is OK to have a relationship with an infected person.

"It's important for people to know that just because someone has an STD, you aren't going to contract it just because you hold their hand . . . it's not the plague or leprosy," she says. Jennifer wants to share her story so that other people in relationships like hers can feel some comfort in "knowing that there is someone out there in [this] situation."

According to Jennifer, both parties have to put one hundred percent into the relationship. "You shouldn't feel the need to continue in a relationship just because you feel bad," she said. Jennifer admits that she takes a risk every time that she and her boyfriend are intimate and acknowledges that it would be a crushing blow for her if she contracted an incurable disease. What allows her to worry less is her boyfriend's ability to deal with his herpes. She has also come to realize that sex is not the most important aspect of a relationship, and that an STD is not a huge limitation on hers.

Jennifer says that giving and receiving support is essential when living with STDs, and the other women echo her sentiment. Cathy's advice to anyone who has tested positive for HIV is: "Reach out, call." Organizations like Women Alive offer HIV-positive women a way to receive strength from other people with HIV, even over the phone.

Marisa says that when you meet other people with herpes, you see how normal they are, and "you are healed mentally." This support helps keep people with herpes from feeling like victims. Marisa refuses to tell the "pity story" because, as she says, "I am not my STD."

Tammy says that meeting other powerful women like Marisa has given her the courage to speak up. She now has casual conversations about herpes in coffee shops. Tammy is not ashamed to promote the Web site because she says that helping people is "bigger than me, bigger than being embarrassed."

Marisa, Tammy, Cathy, and Jennifer can all say that their life has taken a different path than what they had originally intended. Much of their time is dedicated to outreach and STD prevention, stressing both support and individual responsibility. Marisa says that protection comes from loving yourself and saying, "I don't want to have sex yet. This is my body and I have to see [your test results] in writing."

A fortune-teller once told Marisa that she would heal the world, and now Marisa is looking toward her mission. Her goal is to start a nonprofit organization that funds social groups to help people live and love beyond the stigma of having an STD.

When she walks into a bar today, she loves to tell people what she does for a living.

# AN UPSCALE CALL GIRL SPEAKS OUT ON SAFE SEX

Tracy Quan

*When your body is your business, safe sex practices become particularly important, writes Tracy Quan, an upscale call girl and author of* Diary of a Manhattan Call Girl. *In the following selection, Quan explains that the AIDS epidemic, which awoke public awareness about the dangers of sexually transmitted diseases (STDs) and the need for safe sex, was a great benefit to working prostitutes. For example, she observes that before AIDS, clients did not readily accept using condoms, and working prostitutes would have to spend a lot of money on testing for STDs. Unlike nonprofessionals, prostitutes must think about STDs all the time, and although she understands that her friends who are not pros might not want to think about safe sex, Quan feels it is irresponsible and dangerous not to take preventive measures. However, says Quan, not all pros share her safe sex philosophy because some are more interested in profits than safety: Safe sex, these prostitutes argue, takes longer, thus reducing their profit potential.*

South Africa has lately been at the center of the world prostitutes movement. The International Network of Sex Work Projects is currently based in Capetown. And not far from Capetown, the recent 13th International AIDS Conference was held July 9–14, 2000. But whether it occurs in Geneva, Switzerland, or Durban, South Africa, this event is a magnet for sex workers' rights activists and is a must-attend for anyone who plays a leadership role in the world prostitutes movement.

Right now, as I sit in New York, playing hooky from the biggest event of the year, alliances are forming and shifting, dying, reviving. Political love affairs are breaking down. Some are being tenderly nourished. Covert enemies are smiling at each other as they salivate over each other's funding. New factions are sprouting as former enemies are forced to share hotel rooms. Australians are dissing each other to their foreign allies, Latin Americans are making North Americans feel guilty and North Americans (especially from the U.S.) are trying not to offend anyone from Europe or any developing countries.

## The Impact of AIDS

AIDS is a tragedy of epic proportions, claiming millions of lives. But AIDS has also made the prostitutes movement a global one. Before AIDS, the movement sought its alliances among feminists, and this limited our growth. During the 1990s this has changed and most of the important alliances tend to be AIDS related. AIDS is terrible, we all agree, but it helped our movement come of age. Many activist prostitutes have built innovative careers in public health, social and medical research and elsewhere because of AIDS.

In real life, far from the politicized atmosphere of the sex workers summit in Durban, working prostitutes also benefit from the very thing they fear. In the 1980s, when my friends in the life became aware of AIDS, some clients had trouble getting used to condoms. And one working girl I know expressed the problem personally. She told a client: "If you've ever had to sit next to the hospital bed of a friend who is dying of this disease, you'll appreciate the need for a condom!"

Yes, '80s foreplay was sometimes heavy-handed. But she wasn't kidding. One of this girl's best friends from high school, a gay man, had just died.

Later, when just about everyone in our sphere—clients, working girls, madams—had converted to the cause of condoms, she told me: "Thank god for AIDS—when I think of all the men I used to see without condoms, I just can't believe it!"

Her sorrow over a friend who died of AIDS was, is, still real. But AIDS gave her a good reason—an "excuse"—to use a device that had been unfashionable for a while. Condoms made her work a lot safer in general. Risks she had previously taken for granted pre-AIDS now seemed intolerable. Like any other person who has experienced technological improvements on the job, she was amazed at what she had once been able to live with.

Other prostitutes agreed with my friend. It was comforting to know you weren't being exposed to chlamydia, pregnancy or gonorrhea. Men, the selfish beasts, weren't so easily persuaded by the specter of curable ailments or of pregnancies that didn't affect them. The incurable specter of AIDS became a handy angel of guilt hovering over our beds, urging our customers to wear condoms.

Pre-AIDS, when condoms were not always the norm, it was normal to get tested at least monthly for a range of STDs (sexually transmitted diseases). This wasn't just time-consuming, it was expensive. But worth it, of course.

"Before AIDS," one friend reminisced, "I used to spend $200 a month on gonorrhea cultures and lab tests. Once I actually had to get a penicillin shot." And once, she even got pregnant, as a result of the imperfections of the diaphragm method. Condoms have made her life safer and saner by reducing her medical and emotional overhead.

When your body is your portable workstation, you fear for its safety. You're alert to the many bugs, glitches and unwelcome problems that can endanger its health, put you out of work, make you less marketable. For many prostitutes, AIDS is just one of these hazards and it's not even the largest threat in our sex lives.

## Protecting Your Body from Many Health Hazards

Safe sex means more than preventing infection with HIV. It means protecting your cervix from HPV (human papilloma virus) and cancer by using a barrier like a condom or a diaphragm. It means protecting your throat against gonorrhea, guarding against pregnancy, protecting your clients from infections. Nobody wants to expose a customer to an STD.

When it comes to prostitution and illness, it's the transmittable ailments that get all the front-page coverage. But for many hookers, the biggest health problems are work related yet noncontagious. So, safe sex can also mean abstaining from vaginal intercourse—with lovers *or* clients—to reduce the mechanical irritations leading to nonspecific urethritis and recurring bladder infections.

"I had a UTI [urinary tract infection] that was actually caused by my boyfriend—we were having too good a time—and I couldn't work," one girl told me. "My doctor ordered me to stop fucking for *two entire weeks*. I didn't listen to him because I felt better—the infection was gone. And then the problem came back a month later. I lost more time because I was too greedy to give my body a rest."

The second time around, she stuck to oral sex during the recovery period and was able to return to work.

In each case, then, "safe" takes on different meanings. Many readers of my fiction series have asked why fictional call girl Nancy Chan doesn't kiss. Is it, they ask, because kissing is too intimate? Not exactly. Refusing to kiss clients on the mouth is, for many professionals, a form of safe sex.

Many working girls say that kissing increases their chance of catching a cold, and most prostitutes I know worry more about catching a cold than they do about contracting an exotic and deadly virus. The STD problem they've got covered—with condoms—but other bugs are harder to dodge. Many prostitutes say that being exposed at close quarters to so many people is a challenge to the immune system. They fanatically dose themselves with vitamin C and coenzyme Q, keep boxes of homeopathic cold remedies on hand and sleep a lot.

Even though a cold won't kill you, it will put you out of work for a week. Prostitution is demanding: You are required to look and act alert, happy, healthy and pretty at all times. You cannot do this with a runny nose or a sore throat. In some jobs, you might be regarded as a hero for struggling into the office with the remains of a head cold. In this job, you just look desperate.

## A Good Sexual Citizen

When your body is your business, you don't find it insulting to be told about the latest new STD test—you actively want the latest and the best in prevention, detection and (if need be) treatment.

A friend of mine in the business says, "If you don't get an HIV test, if you don't sit down and think about every sex act you perform, you're unprofessional. If you don't use condoms, if you don't get your blood tested, you're an incredible *slob*. It's piggish not to care if you're a pro. But if you're not a pro, it's romantic; it's a sign of your innocence perhaps or your purity."

In 1992, one of my closest friends, an editor in her 20s, was still on the Pill. I knew what this meant: She wasn't using condoms! How relentlessly I nagged her, and how merrily she resisted my finger-wagging warnings. "Oh, I'm just being very fin de siècle [modern] about it," she said, cheerfully. "Besides, I'm not as much of a feminist about this condom thing as you are, Tracy."

That really shut me up, since I regarded myself not as a feminist but as a post-feminist. God, was HIV turning me into one of those preachy militant friends—the kind of female friend who advises you not to lose weight because she fears you'll develop an eating disorder (even though you really need to lose 15 pounds)?

I was somewhat pissed off with her. A prostitute who decides to take risks with her body would be viewed as a social menace in need of rehab, a dangerous vector of disease, perhaps even a felon in some parts of the United States. Only a shameless amateur could get away with this.

It was indeed a very fin de siècle moment: My "virtuous" friend had never disapproved of my sexual conduct, was quite supportive of my right to do it, and I was the scandalized, self-righteous one. I wanted to be a good sexual citizen and she didn't care one way or the other. In reality, I was more preoccupied with sex-based "virtue" than she was. I consoled myself with the thought that I, the responsible sex professional, was taking proper care of my intimate equipment.

## What Is Safe?

But again, the concept of "safe" keeps changing. This year I began to read about the possible dangers posed by monthly ovulation and the likely benefits of the Pill. I was horrified and humbled by the realization that my Pill-taking friend—the self-confessed sexual amateur who'd slept with perhaps seven men in her entire life, who once told me "there has to be a patina of respectability" when she goes to bed with a man—had probably done a better job of protecting her ovaries and her uterus than I had! While practicing safe sex with condoms and reducing one set of risks, I had inadvertently exposed myself to other risks.

I called up a fellow activist, an ex-prostitute with a Ph.D. in public health who frequently gives lectures on how to reduce HIV risk among sex workers. I railed about the possible harm caused by our movement's obsession with HIV—condom-using sex workers are exposing their ovaries to possible cancer for years on end!

"Is it possible that, in some cases, a female prostitute is *more* at risk of contracting ovarian cancer than HIV? That if she had to choose between the Pill and a condom she might, because of her particular style of working, be safer with the Pill?" I asked.

I expected her to cluck disapprovingly. HIV after all is a sacred cow. I didn't know what she would say about the ovarian cancer risk posed by monthly ovulation. Just another crackpot theory?

"Actually," she said, "I think there's something to it. In the Netherlands, a lot of prostitutes use Depo-Provera. Their work schedules aren't interrupted by menstruation and they use condoms, too." She surprised me by agreeing that a sex worker's HIV risk can be grossly exaggerated. But we both felt that saying this too loudly in the prostitutes movement would be perceived as irresponsible.

## A Divide Among Pros

Just as professionals are often divided from "amateurs" by their attitudes toward safe sex, testing and risk, prostitutes themselves are sexually factionalized.

There is the faction that always uses a condom for oral sex. There is the faction that prefers to but sometimes goes without.

There's also a generation gap. Call girls and madams of a certain age, who still embrace the free and easy mores of the '60s and '70s, are often repelled by the idea of performing oral sex with a condom. Or they have trouble taking the idea seriously.

Prostitutes in their 20s and 30s are accustomed to taking extra precautions. They're often impatient with relaxed sexual attitudes. "Forget it!" a friend once said, describing a madam's special request. "Never! It's not worth getting gonorrhea of the throat for $300."

It's commonly accepted that while AIDS is the harbinger, the use of latex protects working girls against less deadly bugs. Despite all the talk of death, the working girl feels she is winning a daily, weekly, hourly battle with mundane things like trichomoniasis, nonspecific vaginal infections, gonorrhea and chlamydia.

But some professionals feel justified in making exceptions. "I have a regular who is so biiiiiig," says another girl. "I just can't get a latex condom onto him. We've tried everything, even the larger latex ones." When she confessed to using a rolled Trojan lambskin, she quickly added, "I put nonoxynol-9 in the tip, just in case." Why, some readers might wonder, doesn't a successful call girl just drop a client if he's too well-endowed to deal with a latex condom? Nobody knows better than she that we're experiencing an economic boom.

"I like him," she shrugs, "and he's really quick. I know latex is the safest and lambskin's kind of risky. But really, I think the risk is minimal."

Safer sex is harder sex. In assessing a client's value, some prostitutes just look at his price. Others realize that a client's true "price" or value isn't just what he pays.

"My safest client," says my friend with the well-endowed client, "is a guy who takes forever in bed. I don't mind because he's so ultrasafe. But he's a lot of work. I feel drained after he leaves. I know he would come so much faster if I took off the damn condom. . . . Sometimes I'm tempted. I could just take that thing off and he'd be done! It's very tempting. But life is full of temptations, isn't it?"

# THE DISEASE INTERVENTION SPECIALIST: FIGHTING THE WAR AGAINST STDS

Sam Stall

In the following selection, Sam Stall describes the day-to-day battles faced by the Disease Intervention Specialist (DIS) of Marion County, Indiana. The DIS team, Stall writes, has had a significant impact on the outbreak of syphilis that spread within the county in 1999. According to Stall, the DIS, also known as a Clap Cop, hits the streets to track and inform those who have been tested whether or not they have contracted a sexually transmitted disease (STD). If the client is infected, DIS team members then recommend treatment and obtain a list of recent sexual partners who also need to be tested. In order to be effective, reports Stall, the DIS must be well trained on the nature and treatment of STDs. In fact, he observes, the DIS often knows more about STDs than some physicians. The DIS faces several challenges; as might be expected, the DIS who must deliver bad news sometimes encounters angry clients or their partners, but equally frustrating is the reaction of parents and partners in denial. However, says Stall, most DIS team members find the rewards worth the challenges. Stall is the editor of *Indianapolis Monthly,* a local news and lifestyle magazine.

One could easily mistake Delaine Young for a Jehovah's Witness. Day after day, dressed in clothes befitting a Sunday-school teacher, she visits the homes of strangers to deliver messages most don't want to hear. She's rarely welcomed, and some of her targets go to great lengths to avoid her. "I usually start knocking on doors at 9 A.M.," she says. "By then you don't get cussed out too badly if you wake people up."

But when Young shows up on someone's porch, rest assured it's not to discuss hellfire and damnation. The only fire that concerns her is the burning sensation brought on by sexually transmitted diseases (STDs). Young is a Disease Intervention Specialist (DIS) for the Marion

County Health Department—one of a small band of shock troops on the front line of the county's struggle to contain Indy's [Indianapolis] massive, widely publicized syphilis outbreak.

Since 1999, when Marion County, Indiana, was revealed to have the highest syphilis rate in the nation, Indianapolis public health officials have built up a massive roster of programs to deal with the problem—everything from new STD screening efforts at area emergency rooms to a sprawling network of civic organizations called the Stamp Out Syphilis Coalition. But the big victories have been won by the smallest group, the DIS team. The efforts of this toothpick force are the primary reason the local syphilis rate declined by roughly a quarter in 2000. "I'd say the No. 1 key to addressing this epidemic has to be our disease intervention specialists," says Marion County Health Department director Dr. Virginia Caine. "It's a thankless job. They do a tremendous amount of work, but people have no idea of the value of what they do."

## Hitting the Streets

The DIS team's approach to disease control couldn't be more low-tech—or indispensable. Operatives track down all people in Marion County and the seven surrounding counties who test positive for syphilis; make sure they receive treatment; obtain a list of their recent sex partners; and try to make sure each of those is tested and treated—every single one. They do the same for some gonorrhea and chlamydia patients, plus those newly diagnosed with HIV. And to make things even trickier, all client names must be kept strictly confidential.

DIS squads have been around for decades. They've operated across the nation under various names, but usually under the auspices (and on the payroll) of the Centers for Disease Control and Prevention (CDC) headquarters in Atlanta. The central Indiana contingent works out of the Bell Flower Clinic, the city's massive downtown STD treatment facility. Currently there are only 11 on the team, along with two supervisors and Duane Wilmot, the program coordinator. Wilmot works directly for the CDC; three of his troops are funded by the Marion County Health Department, while the rest are paid by the Indiana State Department of Health using CDC grant money.

The nine Clap Cops, as the DIS operatives facetiously call themselves, who are assigned to regular street duty must canvass a hefty chunk of central Indiana. In a perfect world, most of their business—informing people of test results, then arranging for treatment—could be accomplished by phone. But when a considerable portion of your clientele consists of prostitutes, drug addicts, the indigent and wanted criminals, simply giving them a ring can be problematic. So when all else fails, DIS operatives make like Joe Friday [a character in the 1950s police drama, *Dragnet*] and hit the streets.

Young, like her cohorts, divides her time between desk duty at the

Bell Flower Clinic and field work. On this particular day she'll spend her morning driving from one end of the city to the other, tracking down patients.

She carries today's field reports in "the pouch," a small black notebook that also contains several pages of photos of infected penises and vaginas. When a DIS tries to help patients understand the nature of their ailment, those pictures are worth a thousand words. Young also hauls around a big cloth bag full of paperwork, but rarely removes it from her car—it might jeopardize her clients' anonymity, since the letters STD are emblazoned on the side. Not that her contacts, whom she occasionally encounters in public, necessarily grant her as much discretion. Once as he stood in line at a store, a former patient spotted her and said cheerily, "Hey, there's the syphilis lady."

## The Hot Zones

At a little past 8:30 A.M., The Syphilis Lady makes her first stop of the day—a College Avenue liquor store where she tapes up a large public health poster. This is prime real estate for such educational materials, because it falls within one of the four near northside zip codes designated as "hot zones" for syphilis, along with two "warm zones." "When you figure those six areas, you account for 68 percent of the cases of primary and secondary syphilis," says DIS coordinator Wilmot. But suburbanites tempted to dismiss the epidemic as an inner city problem should remember that more than 30 percent of cases fall outside Center Township. In fact, if you tacked a map of central Indiana to a tree and fired a shotgun at it, the dispersal pattern would mimic that of reported syphilis cases—a huge number of hits in the near-downtown bull's-eye, with individual bits of buckshot straying as far afield as Anderson and Mooresville.

Blame the long reach of the disease on your Friendly Neighborhood Crack Whore and her clients. An infected prostitute can spread syphilis far and wide—especially if some of her clients drive in from the sticks. Every out-of-towner who stops by for a quickie goes home with a parting "gift"—one that he will probably share with his wife and/or girlfriend. "If you pull up at this intersection (22nd and College) and hesitate, you'll have someone approach you," Young says. Even this early. When she made several visits to one hot zone, a suspicious hooker working a particular corner felt the need to warn Young not to "come on my turf."

Perhaps she drove by so many times because she was lost. Each day's batch of DIS appointments is a no-rhyme-or-reason collection of people who couldn't or wouldn't be reached by phone. Though she prints out directions to unfamiliar locations, Young can still spend many precious minutes rolling down alleys and side streets, looking for addresses.

This morning, Young spends more than 10 minutes prowling the Highland-Brookside area before finding the desired address—and learning that her quarry, a girl who tested positive for chlamydia, isn't home. So Young drops off an envelope stamped CONFIDENTIAL in big, red letters. Inside is a cryptic request for the girl to contact her because "a serious matter concerning your health has come to our attention." That's as specific as DIS notes can get without compromising the recipient's all-important right to privacy.

## Focusing on Syphilis

Getting blown off by clients is all in a day's work. Nevertheless, DIS agents manage to interview about 95 percent of the early-stage syphilis cases that come to their attention. They're the most important to locate, because they're the most infectious. The DIS team would like to hunt down the carriers of other common STDs, but the numbers are against them. Last year they tackled 433 cases of early-stage syphilis. However, reported gonorrhea cases numbered almost 4,000 and chlamydia almost 7,000. "With a staff of 11, it's impossible to interview every single one," says Young's boss, Wilmot. "We will interview everybody who comes to Bell Flower Clinic and is treated for gonorrhea and chlamydia. But there's no way we can follow up with everyone. We'd need a staff of 500 to make a dent in that."

Even the relatively more manageable list of syphilis patients can be a handful. While DIS operatives track down almost all early-stage carriers, they're able to locate, examine and interview only about 60 percent of those people's sex partners—any one of whom could also be infected. Casting such a wide net occasionally brings in some familiar-looking fish. Some of the DIS operatives have seen friends and members of their church congregations come into the Bell Flower Clinic for treatment. "I also remember going to an amusement park, and the gal who was putting my 3-year-old daughter on the kiddy ride was one of my patients," Wilmot says.

## Delivering Bad News

On this sunny morning, Young would settle for seeing anyone—familiar or not. After striking out on her first two home visits, she heads to an eastside apartment complex for what promises to be the day's main event—the delivery of the results of an HIV test. This is the final bit of fallout from what Young describes as the biggest dustup she's ever encountered over such a case.

It began several days earlier, when she visited a woman's house to inform her in person (standard procedure with all HIV positive patients who won't or can't come to the clinic to hear the results) that her test for the virus was positive. But the house was full of friends and relatives, and the woman herself was in the midst of having sex with a man. After Young—who is infamous among her DIS colleagues for her uncanny knack for dropping in on people busy doing the deed—broke the news, the patient nonchalantly told the assembled throng. "Everybody started screaming and crying," she says. "We did a lot of counseling. I think we stayed there about four-and-a-half hours."

Probably the most surprised person was the woman's lover, whom Young is visiting today with the results of his HIV test. She stops by the second-floor apartment he named as his address and knocks repeatedly on the dented steel door. But the only response emanates from inside the next-door residence: a gruff male voice that shouts for the DIS to "stop banging on that g——d door."

Young trudges to a nearby building to drop off a letter for a woman who tested positive for syphilis, then goes back to the original apartment and tries again. This time, after only a couple more knocking bouts, she gains admission to the dimly lit interior. Two men sit on a threadbare couch, watching television. When Young asks after her quarry, she's pointed to a bedroom far down an unlit hall.

The DIS dutifully soldiers on, peeking into the room and finding not a young man but a middle-aged woman. Taking this in stride, Young identifies herself and inquires where her patient might be found.

"Is he positive?" the woman asks matter-of-factly.

Of course Young can't answer. She merely asks the woman to have the man call her when he shows up.

The agent returns to her car, but before she can pull away she spots her test subject nonchalantly driving past in his own vehicle. Did they miss each other or did he dodge her? It could be either. It's not uncommon for people to duck the DIS—sometimes simply because they don't want to hear bad news. But Young isn't worried about this particular case. Curiosity, she figures, will soon get the better of him. "That's another reason why we don't tell results to other people," she says. "Because now he'll be wondering."

The HIV trip sets the tone for a frustrating morning. Young visits the home of a gonorrhea patient but finds no one there, then at 10:30 A.M. hits the last known location of another gonorrhea sufferer, only to find the apartment vacant. Not for the first time, the DIS has been deceived by a bogus address. Now someone will have to check with the woman's doctor, sift through computer records and consult other agents for leads on her location. Sooner or later they'll find her.

## Learning to Be a Clap Cop

Knowledge of human nature, coupled with old-fashioned detective work, helps the DIS track down their targets. The current crop of agents boasts degrees in everything from sociology to criminal justice, but before they hit the street they must also master a CDC training program covering all aspects of field work. "By the time you go through it, you probably know as much as many medical people about the diseases—all the tests and treatments, incubation periods, complications," Wilmot says. Next comes a two-week CDC course covering everything from case management techniques to interviewing skills, along with training on drawing blood and handling HIV cases. And all of this is merely a prelude to months of on-the-job training. "The misconception is that you can hire somebody right off the street and have them doing this in two or three weeks," says veteran DIS Coya Campbell. "But you can't even do it in six months. You need a year."

Though the DIS operatives sometimes act like detectives, they have no cop-like enforcement powers. If someone infected with syphilis refuses treatment, won't provide the names of sex partners or won't agree to stop infecting others, there's nothing a DIS can do about it. Young's all-time promiscuity champ was a prostitute who entertained 99 partners (that she could recall) within a year. "She actually refused to identify them, because she said that was part of her commitment to her people," she says.

Eventually, after repeated pleas, the prostitute gave up the names of a handful of her "people," but only because of the ironclad DIS guarantee of anonymity. If you're tested for an STD, the agents can't share the results with anyone but you, and if you provide them with a list of your possibly-infected sex partners, they won't tell them by whom they were named. It's absolutely necessary if the organization is to have any credibility on the street, though occasionally the rule of confidentiality is put to unsavory use. Once a woman who infected her partner with gonorrhea decided to pretend that he had infected her. And since Young was sworn to secrecy as to who did what to whom, she couldn't say a word about the frame-up.

## Anger and Denial

Informing people that they are positive for HIV is emotionally draining, but calls concerning syphilis or gonorrhea (which, once identified, are both easily curable) can take on the aura of soap operas. That goes double if the person being informed is married to the person whose extracurricular activities brought the disease home. Of course the DIS can't tell a spouse that he or she was infected by a philandering mate, but if the victim is monogamous, figuring it out rarely takes long. In such cases Young simply delivers the bad news and escapes before the crockery flies. "I had someone who spread it to several other people, yet was also engaged to be married in two weeks," she says. "And the person he was getting married to didn't know."

But those complications pale before cases in which teenagers are involved. Since the DIS confidentiality rule applies to anyone over 12, the agents must inform the kid but not the parents. "How would you feel if someone came to talk to your teenage child and said they couldn't tell you what it was about?" Young says. "I had one mother scream at me over the phone and tell me, 'I don't know why you left this [notification letter] at my house. My daughter does not have sex. Don't leave any more of that stuff here.'"

Walking away, however, isn't an option, no matter how much a parent or other adult might want to ignore the situation. Young and other DIS agents occasionally shake their heads at the disconnect between the reality and perception of teen sex. She recalls one youth minister who objected to her leaving condoms and STD information at his meeting area—until she pointed out that several infected teenagers admitted they hooked up with their sex partners at his gatherings.

## The Risks and Rewards

Though her bloodhound work takes her to some of the city's roughest neighborhoods, Young says she rarely feels physically threatened. If she does—like the time she tried to drop off a notification at a house where eight men loitered on the front porch, drinking—she clears out. "I just walked past as if I was looking for something else," she says. Once in a while, however, trouble comes looking for her. "I was interviewing a woman who turned out to be a parole violator, and right in the middle of it the cops burst through the door, guns out," she recalls. "I told them I was from the health department and they said, 'Sorry. We messed up your interview, didn't we?'"

Sometimes it's enough to make her question her calling. But when things get rough, the occasional thank-yous from clients help, as does the undeniable fact that all this door knocking makes a difference. "I'm often asked how I can go into people's houses and ask about their sex lives," Young says. "Well, it's really about the infection. If people need treatment, we want to make sure they get it."

As the clock inches toward 11 A.M., Delaine Young heads back to the office to grab some lunch before her afternoon desk shift at the Bell Flower Clinic. There, she'll gauge the success of her morning by the number of people who contact her to ask why she stopped by. If all those notification letters bring in four fresh calls, she'll consider it worthwhile.

## Tracking the Hard Cases

While Young spent the morning on the street, her fellow DIS, Dan Brooks, worked in the clinic interviewing patients and handling other sundry duties. Now he'll pass the afternoon cruising around, tracking down hard cases.

At 12:30 P.M., Brooks, armed with dossiers for eight patients, hits the road. He and Young couldn't be more different. She's a middle-aged black woman, he's a middle-aged white man who might as well have "Narc" tattooed on his forehead. It's hard to imagine anyone in the hot zone even opening their door to him, let alone giving a detailed account of their sex life. "I think it can hurt because I don't think people are as open when they talk to me," says the seven-year DIS. "A white guy in a black car is going to stick out in certain areas, whereas if you're black and working primarily in a black area, people might feel more comfortable."

On his first run he serves as backup for a female agent who visits a largely abandoned public housing project to draw blood for a syphilis test. During the procedure, the patient, a woman in her 30s, sits on her couch, shaking her head in disbelief at her predicament. Taking blood is a common DIS activity—so common that Brooks has even done it in the street, taking samples from people who stuck their arms out of cars. "Once I talked to a kid who didn't want his parents to know we were going to draw blood," he recalls. "So I pretended I was interviewing him for a job. We went into his bedroom and I drew his blood there. They never knew what happened."

During the syphilis outbreak DIS agents have occasionally canvassed entire hot-zone neighborhoods, offering blood screenings to all comers. They staffed information tables at gay bath houses. But while promiscuous sex plays a major role in the epidemic, the real driver is drugs. Things heated up a couple of years ago when the crack trade hit the city in a big way. "If you have people using crack and they need to get money, one of the things they're going to fall into is having sex," Brooks says. "So if you have more crack, you're probably going to have more prostitution."

And more syphilis-infected prostitutes. DIS workers say they first perceived the looming epidemic a couple of years ago, when a large number of infected men reported contact with hookers, some of whom were so desperate for their next fix that they would do anything for cash. In one case, a cook at a local fried chicken establishment was fired for getting serviced by prostitutes in the men's room in exchange for two-piece chicken dinners.

Nothing so bizarre is on this day's itinerary, however. Brooks spends his field time in the city's heart, trundling down bumpy secondary roads. "This car has seen its share of alleys," he says of his ride. "I had an old, beat-up car, but I pretty much drove it to death. It's always better to have a work car and a real car. If you have a junker, you can park it anywhere and you don't really care what happens to it." At the house of a chlamydia patient he leaves an envelope with the subject's understandably curious teenage son. Then Brooks tries to contact another woman who's been tested for chlamydia but not treated. When no one comes to her apartment door (which bears the marks of a recent crowbar assault), he leaves yet another envelope at her mail box.

## The Unavoidable Obstacles

Spending the afternoon as a glorified mail man isn't much fun for a DIS. Dealing with doctors can also be troublesome, but it's an unavoidable part of the job. All local syphilis cases, even those being handled by private physicians, are reported to and monitored by the DIS team. Because syphilis is easy to miss (some doctors mistake its telltale skin rashes for an allergic reaction) and many physicians have never seen a case, the DIS often must offer advice on the latest treatments. Not surprisingly, some health care providers take exception to being second-guessed by a mere civil servant. "We're there as a safety net, in case it gets misdiagnosed," Brooks says. "You may be double-checking to make sure the treatment is right. If it's wrong, then you have to put your diplomacy to work to let them know that maybe that's not the right treatment." If a problem with a physician persists, someone from the Bell Flower Clinic with a medical degree may call to intervene.

At 2:30 P.M. Brooks pulls into yet another apartment complex to look for a woman who was treated by a private doctor for syphilis symptoms but, oddly, never got tested to learn definitively if she had the disease. The DIS would like to have her tested and get a list of her sex partners, but when he knocks on the door he's greeted by a woman who says the person he seeks hasn't lived there in a year. A quick check at the apartment office confirms this, sending one more case back to the drawing board.

Next comes the oddest call of the day—and a prime example of the bramble of misinformation and obstruction that DIS reps must force their way through in order to help people. Brooks visits another apartment complex, seeking a young girl who's been exposed to gonorrhea. Incredibly, he finds himself knocking on the very same door that Young visited that morning, looking for her HIV-test subject.

This time the man Young sought answers. Behind him on the threadbare couch sit several other people, none of whom was there that morning. But though the HIV-test man is home, the girl with gonorrhea isn't. Brooks asks for her to call, then departs, leaving the man in suspense about his own HIV test (which was negative). Brooks couldn't have helped the man even if he'd asked. It isn't his case.

A screenwriter couldn't have provided a better example of how circumstance and occasional subterfuge can stay these couriers from the swift completion of their appointed rounds. Brooks ends the day by trying to find a syphilis sufferer whose last address turns out to be another empty apartment. At 4:30 P.M., shortly after dropping off notes for two chlamydia patients, he heads back to the barn. "It's so much cooler when they do stuff like this on *Law and Order*," he says. "They leave out the parts where they're knocking on doors and nobody answers."

The DIS crew would love to leave out that part, too. But their willingness to pound the pavement, combined with their low profile, is what makes them so effective. Street work may be tedious, thankless and occasionally dangerous, but it's the only way to get the job done. "If there was another way, then I think they'd try to do it," Brooks says. "But you pretty much have to put someone on the street. It's like taking over a city in a war. You have to go house by house."

# ORGANIZATIONS TO CONTACT

The editors have compiled the following list of organizations concerned with the issues presented in this book. Descriptions are derived from materials provided by the organizations. All have publications or information available for interested readers. The list was compiled on the date of publication of the present volume; names, addresses, phone and fax numbers, and e-mail/Internet addresses may change. Be aware that many organizations take several weeks or longer to respond to inquiries, so allow as much time as possible.

### Academy for Educational Development (AED)
1825 Connecticut Ave. NW, Washington, DC 20009-5721
(202) 884-8000 • fax: (202) 884-8400
e-mail: admindc@aed.org • website: www.aed.org

Founded in 1961, AED is a nonprofit organization committed to improving people's lives and solving critical social problems, including the spread of sexually transmitted diseases (STDs), through education, research, training, policy analysis, and program development. The academy advocates the use of social marketing, including the use of mass media, to communicate on public health problems such as STDs and promote behavior changes. AED publishes a semiannual newsletter, the *Academy News,* and the *Journal of Health Communication,* current issues of which are available on its website as well as information on AED programs and projects. The AED website also provides access to books on STD prevention, including *Adolescents and HIV Disease: Defining the Problem and Its Prevention.*

### Advocates for Youth
1025 Vermont Ave. NW, Suite 200, Washington, DC 20005
(202) 347-5700 • fax: (202) 347-2263
e-mail: info@advocatesforyouth.org • website: www.advocatesforyouth.org

The goal of Advocates for Youth is to create programs and advocate policies that help young people make informed and responsible decisions about their reproductive and sexual health. To change what it believes are archaic policies and promote its core values—rights, respect, and responsibility, the organization provides information, training, and strategic assistance to youth-serving organizations, policy makers, youth activists, and the media. On its website, Advocates for Youth provides access to lesson plans for educators and information and guidance for parents and teens. The site also provides facts and statistics and current research on sexually transmitted diseases (STDs) and news on public health policies that affect young people around the world.

### The Alan Guttmacher Institute (AGI)
120 Wall St., 21st Floor, New York, NY 10005
(212) 248-1111 • fax: (212) 248-1951
e-mail: info@guttmacher.org • website: www.agi-usa.org

AGI is a nonprofit organization focused on sexual and reproductive health research, policy analysis, and public education. The goal of AGI is to protect the reproductive choices of all women and men in the United States and throughout the world and support their ability to obtain information and services to safeguard their health and exercise their responsibilities in regard to sexual behavior, reproduction, and family planning. AGI publishes *Family Planning Perspectives, International Family Planning Perspectives,* the *Guttmacher Report on*

*Public Policy,* and special reports on sexual and reproductive health and rights. On its website, the institute provides articles on reproductive health issues, including sexually transmitted diseases (STDs), online versions of recent AGI publications, and a search engine to access its periodical archives.

### American Social Health Association (ASHA)
PO Box 13827, Research Triangle Park, NC 27709
(919) 361-8400 • fax: (919) 361-8425
website: www.ashastd.org

ASHA is a nongovernmental organization that develops and delivers information about STDs to help community organizations communicate about risk, transmission, prevention, testing, and treatment of sexually transmitted diseases (STDs). The goal of the association is to stop STDs and their harmful consequences by improving public awareness, providing patient education and support, and promoting strong health care policies. On its website, ASHA provides resources to answer questions, finds referrals, join self-help groups, and access in-depth information on STDs, including the newsletters *the helper* (concerning genital herpes) and *HPV News.* The website also provides access to ASHA pamphlets, including "Loving Safely: What You Need to Know About STDs" and "A Practical Guide for the Tongue-Tied: How to Talk About STDs" and books, including *Managing Herpes: How to Live and Love with a Chronic STD.*

### Association of Reproductive Health Professionals (ARHP)
2401 Pennsylvania Ave. NW, Suite 350, Washington, DC 20037-1718
(202) 466-3825 • fax: (202) 466-3826
e-mail: arhp@arhp.org • website: www.arhp.org

Founded in 1963, ARHP is a nonprofit, national medical organization dedicated to educating physicians, other health care providers, patients, and the public about important reproductive health issues, including sexually transmitted diseases (STDs). ARHP's goal is to provide reproductive health education and services, conduct research, and influence health policy. On its website, ARHP provides access to information and current research on STDs and headlines on ARHP programs and reproductive health issues.

### Centers for Disease Control and Prevention (CDC)
### National Center for HIV, STD, and TB Prevention (NCHSTP)
### Division of Sexually Transmitted Diseases (DSTD)
1600 Clifton Rd., Atlanta, GA 30333
(404) 639-3534 • (800) 311-3435 • fax: (404) 639-8910
National STD Hotline: (800) 227-8922
e-mail: nchstp@cdc.gov • website: www.cdc.gov

The CDC is a federal agency created to protect the public health. The DSTD provides national leadership through research, policy development, and support of effective services to prevent STDs and their complications. The division conducts surveillance, research, and program evaluation related to STDs and assists states and selected localities in reaching those at risk for infection. The DSTD also collaborates with community-based organizations to enhance STD prevention awareness. On its website, the DSTD provides access to recent news on STD treatment and prevention and articles about STDs in CDC publications, including recent issues of *Morbidity and Mortality Weekly Report (MMWR)* and *Tracking the Hidden Epidemics, Trends in STDs in the United States 2000.*

## Family Health International (FHI)
PO Box 13950, Research Triangle Park, NC 27709
(919) 544-7040 • fax: (919) 544-7261
e-mail: services@fhi.org • website: www.fhi.org

Established in 1971, FHI is a nonprofit organization committed to helping women and men obtain access to safe, effective, and affordable family planning services and methods, preventing the spread of HIV/AIDS and sexually transmitted diseases (STDs), and improving the health of women and children. Working in collaboration with a worldwide network of government agencies, research institutions, nongovernmental organizations, and private sector entities, FHI advances the public health through research, training, and education. FHI publications include scientific journal articles, fact sheets, books, reports, training manuals, and multimedia materials, some of which are available on its website. Also on its website, FHI provides access to current issues of its semi-annual periodical *Impact on HIV* and its quarterly bulletin *Network*, which includes reports on research and programs to prevent STDs.

## Kaiser Family Foundation
2400 Sand Hill Rd., Menlo Park, CA 94025
(650) 854-9400 • fax: (650) 854-4800
website: www.kff.org

The Henry J. Kaiser Family Foundation is an independent philanthropy that focuses on major health care issues facing the nation, including the STD epidemic. The foundation serves as a source of facts and analysis for policy makers, the media, the health care community, and the general public. On its website, the foundation provides health policy and public health information, including foundation publications such as *What Teens Know and Don't (but Should) About Sexually Transmitted Diseases, The Tip of the Iceberg: How Big Is the STD Epidemic in the U.S.?* and *Talking About STDs with Health Professionals: Women's Experiences.*

## National Institute of Allergy and Infectious Diseases (NIAID)
## National Institutes of Health (NIH)
Building 31, Room 7A-50, 31 Center Drive MSC 2520, Bethesda, MD 20892-2520
(301) 496-5717
website: www.niaid.nih.gov

NIAID provides the major support for scientists conducting research aimed at developing better ways to diagnose, treat, and prevent many infectious, immunologic, and allergic diseases that afflict people worldwide. The Division of AIDS conducts and supports research on the pathogenesis of human immunodeficiency virus (HIV), which causes AIDS, develops new drug therapies, conducts clinical trials of promising experimental drugs, carries out epidemiologic studies to assess the impact of HIV on the populations most severely affected by the epidemic, and develops and tests HIV vaccines. NIAID also supports research on sexually transmitted diseases (STDs) to develop better diagnostic tests, improved treatments, and effective vaccines. On its website, NIAID provides access to fact sheets and brochures on the most common STDs, including chlamydia, genital herpes, gonorrhea, human papillomavirus, syphilis, and pelvic inflammatory disease. The NIAID website also provides access to news releases on current research, prevention strategies, and treatments, and provides links to MEDLINE, the National Library of Medicine's bibliographic database, and current NIAID clinical trials and other NIH studies.

### National Women's Health Information Center (NWHIC)
Office on Women's Health
US Department of Health and Human Services
8550 Arlington Blvd., Suite 300, Fairfax, VA 22031
(800) 994-9662 • TYY: (888) 220-5446
website: http://4woman.org

The goal of the NWHIC is to provide current, reliable, commercial, and cost-free health information to women and their families. The information center provides access to federal and other women's health information resources on health issues including sexually transmitted diseases (STDs). The NWHIC website is a health information and referral center for women, answering frequently asked questions and providing access to its newsletter *Healthy Women Today* and federal and nongovernmental publications, including "An Introduction to Sexually Transmitted Diseases" and "Challenge of STD Prevention in the United States." The website also provides daily news stories and access to archives in "Women's Health News Today."

### Planned Parenthood Federation of America (PPFA)
810 Seventh Ave., New York, NY 10019
(212) 261-4729 • fax: (212) 247-6342
e-mail: communications@ppfa.org • website: www.plannedparenthood.org

PPFA is a voluntary reproductive health care organization founded by Margaret Sanger in 1916 as America's first birth control clinic. The federation believes that it is the fundamental right of each individual to manage his or her fertility, regardless of income, marital status, race, ethnicity, sexual orientation, age, national origin, or residence. One of the goals of PPFA is to provide reproductive and health care services that enhance understanding of the implications of human sexuality, including sexual health. On its website, PPFA provides fact sheets and information on specific sexually transmitted diseases (STDs), guides to healthy and safe sex, and archives of its newsletters, which include *Educator's Update, Clergy Voices,* and the e-mail newsletter *teenwire.com.*

# BIBLIOGRAPHY

## Books

| | |
|---|---|
| Peter L. Allen | *The Wages of Sin: Sex and Disease, Past and Present.* Chicago: University of Chicago Press, 2000. |
| Elizabeth Carter | *Everything You Need to Know About Human Papillomavirus.* New York: Rosen Publishing Group, 2001. |
| R. Eng and William T. Butler, eds. | *The Hidden Epidemic: Confronting Sexually Transmitted Diseases.* Washington, DC: National Academy Press, 1997. |
| Gregory T. Everson and Hedy Weinberg | *Living with Hepatitis B: A Survivor's Guide.* Long Island City, NY: Hatherleigh Press, 2002. |
| Gregory Henderson and Batya Yasgur | *Women at Risk: The HPV Epidemic and Your Cervical Health.* New York: Avery/Penguin Putnam, 2002. |
| King K. Holmes, ed. | *Sexually Transmitted Diseases.* New York: McGraw-Hill, 1999. |
| Melissa K. Hough and Julie A. Poppe | *Sexually Transmitted Diseases: A Policymaker's Guide and Summary of State Laws.* Denver: National Conference of State Legislatures, 1998 |
| Edward O. Laumann and Robert T. Michael, eds. | *Sex, Love, and Health in America: Private Choices and Public Policies.* Chicago: University of Chicago Press, 2000. |
| Evelyn Lerman | *Safer Sex: The New Morality.* Buena Park, CA: Morning Glory Press, 2000. |
| Janet Majure | *AIDS: Diseases and People.* Berkeley Heights, NJ: Enslow Publishers, 1998. |
| Susan Moore | *Youth, Aids, and Sexually Transmitted Diseases.* New York: Routledge, 1997. |
| Jeffery A. Nevid | *Choices: Sex in the Age of STDs.* Boston: Allyn & Bacon, 1997. |
| Stephen L. Sacks | *The Truth About Herpes.* Seattle: Gordon Soules, 1997. |
| Lawrence Raymond Stanberry | *Understanding Herpes.* Jackson: University Press of Mississippi, 1998. |
| Lawrence Raymond Stanberry and David I. Bernstein, eds. | *Sexually Transmitted Diseases: Vaccines, Prevention, and Control.* San Diego: Academic Press, 2000. |
| Diane Yancey | *STDs: What You Don't Know Can Hurt You.* Breckenridge, CO: Twenty First-Century Books, 2002. |

## Periodicals

| | |
|---|---|
| American Academy of Family Physicians | "What Should I Know About Genital Herpes?" *American Family Physician*, March 15, 2000. |

| | |
|---|---|
| Jim Bloor | "The Four Faces of Chlamydia," *Men's Fitness*, May 1999. |
| Loretta Brabin | "Hormonal Markers of Susceptibility to Sexually Transmitted Infections: Are We Taking Them Seriously?" *British Medical Journal*, August 18, 2001. |
| Jennifer Braunschweiger | "The New Sexual Taboo," *Self*, November 2001. |
| Willard Cates Jr. | "Treating STDs to Help Control HIV Infection," *Contemporary OB/GYN*, October 2001. |
| Harrell Chesson, Paul Harrison, and William J. Kassler | "Sex Under the Influence: The Effect of Alcohol Policy on Sexually Transmitted Disease Rates in the United States," *The Journal of Law and Economics*, April 2000. |
| Committee on Adolescence | "Condom Use by Adolescents," *Pediatrics*, June 2001. |
| Stephanie A. Crockett | "Doing It to Death," *Essence*, July 1997. |
| Jan Farrington | "STDs and AIDS: What Teens Need to Know," *Current Health 1*, November 2001. |
| Gayle Forman | "STDs From A to A?" *Seventeen*, September 2001. |
| J. Dennis Fortenberry | "Unveiling the Hidden Epidemic of Sexually Transmitted Diseases," *Journal of the American Medical Association*, February 13, 2002. |
| Ryan Gierach | "Syphilis Cases Still Rising," *The Advocate*, September 25, 2001. |
| Erik L. Goldman | "Arthritis Before Age 30 May Signal Gonorrhea," *Family Practice News*, February 15, 2000. |
| Zondra Hughes | "Risky Business: What's Behind the Surge in Sexually Transmitted Diseases," *Ebony*, January 2000. |
| Leslie Laurence | "Special Report: Sexual Health Emergency," *Glamour*, August 1998. |
| William M. Lee | "Hepatitis B Virus Infection," *New England Journal of Medicine*, December 11, 1997. |
| Hallie Levine | "Should You Come Clean About Your Sexual History?" *Cosmopolitan*, August 2001. |
| James A. McGregor | "Diagnosing and Treating STDs in Young Women," *Contemporary Pediatrics*, February 2001. |
| Joe S. McIlhaney Jr. and Debra Haffner | "Are 'Abstinence-Only' Sex-Education Programs Good for Teenagers?" *CQ Researcher*, July 10, 1998. |
| Jodi Godfrey Meisler | "Toward Optimal Health: The Experts Discuss Herpes," *Journal of Women's Health & Gender-Based Medicine*, October 2000. |
| Mary Jane Minkin and Toby Hanlon | "STDs: A Risk in Your 50s?" *Prevention*, April 2001. |
| Adina Nack | "Damaged Goods: Women Managing the Stigma of STDs," *Deviant Behavior*, March/April 2000. |

| Mark Nichols | "Dangerous Liaisons: Chlamydia Can Cause Infertility or Ectopic Pregnancies," *Maclean's*, October 12, 1998. |

J. Rosenberg — "Condoms Reduce Women's Risk of Herpes Infection, but Do Not Protect Men," *International Family Planning Perspectives*, December 2001.

Richard H. Schwarz — "How STDs Affect Your Pregnancy," *American Baby*, October 2001.

Michel Thuriaux and Suzanne Cherney — "AIDS Affects Us All," *World Health*, January/Feburary 1997.

Pat Wingert — "Promise's Story," *Newsweek*, June 3, 2002.

## Websites

American Medical Association — Sexually Transmitted Disease Information Center. *JAMA Women's Health: Journal of the American Medical Association*. www.ama-assn.org.

Boston University School of Medicine — "Sexually Transmitted Diseases," *Medvalet/COHIS*. www.bu.edu.

Richard B. Roberts, M.D. — "Pathophysiology: Sexually Transmitted Diseases," *CUMC: Courseware*, Cornell University Medical College. http://edcenter.med.cornell.edu.

University of Arizona — "Human Biology: Sexually Transmitted Diseases (STDs)," *The Biology Project*. www.biology.arizona.edu.

# INDEX